BUSINESS ISSUES, COMPETITION AND ENTREPRENEURSHIP

WORKFORCE DIVERSITY IN THE FINANCIAL SECTOR

BUSINESS ISSUES, COMPETITION AND ENTREPRENEURSHIP

Additional books in this series can be found on Nova's website under the Series tab.

Additional E-books in this series can be found on Nova's website under the E-book tab.

BUSINESS ISSUES, COMPETITION AND ENTREPRENEURSHIP

WORKFORCE DIVERSITY IN THE FINANCIAL SECTOR

EMILY CRUZ
AND
DEREK HOUGHTON
EDITORS

nova publishers
New York

For permission to use material from this book please contact us:
Telephone 631-231-7269; Fax 631-231-8175
Web Site: http://www.novapublishers.com

Library of Congress Cataloging-in-Publication Data

ISBN: 978-1-62808-442-9

Published by Nova Science Publishers, Inc. † New York

CONTENTS

PREFACE

As the U.S. workforce has become increasingly diverse, many private- and public-sector entities recognize the importance of recruiting and retaining minorities and women for management-level positions to improve their business. The 2007-2009 financial crisis has renewed questions about commitment within the financial services industry (e.g., banking and securities) to workforce diversity. The Dodd-Frank Act required that eight federal financial agencies and the Federal Reserve Banks implement provisions to support workforce and contractor diversity. This book reviews the trends and practices implemented since the beginning of the financial crisis and examines (1) workforce diversity in the financial services industry, the federal financial agencies, and Reserve Banks from 2007 through 2011 and (2) the efforts of the agencies and Reserve Banks to implement workforce diversity practices under the Dodd-Frank Act, including contracting.

Chapter 1 – As the U.S. workforce has become increasingly diverse, many private- and public-sector entities recognize the importance of recruiting and retaining minorities and women for management-level positions to improve their business. The 2007-2009 financial crisis has renewed questions about commitment within the financial services industry (e.g., banking and securities) to workforce diversity. The Dodd-Frank Act required that eight federal financial agencies and the Federal Reserve Banks implement provisions to support workforce and contractor diversity. GAO was asked to review trends and practices since the beginning of the financial crisis. This report examines (1) workforce diversity in the financial services industry, the federal financial agencies, and Reserve Banks, from 2007 through 2011 and (2) efforts of the agencies and Reserve Banks to implement workforce diversity practices under the Dodd-Frank Act, including contracting. GAO analyzed federal datasets and documents and interviewed industry representatives and officials from the federal financial agencies and Reserve Banks.

Chapter 2 – As the U.S. workforce has become increasingly diverse, many private and public sector organizations have recognized the importance of recruiting and retaining minority and women candidates for key positions. However, previous congressional hearings have raised concerns about a lack of diversity at the management level in the financial services industry, which provides services that are essential to the continued growth and economic recovery of the country. The recent financial crisis has renewed concerns about the financial services industry's commitment to workforce diversity.

This testimony discusses findings from a June 2006 GAO report (GAO-06-617), February 2008 testimony (GAO-08-445T), and more recent work on diversity in the financial services industry. Specifically, GAO assesses (1) what the available data show about diversity at the management level from 1993 through 2008 and (2) steps that the industry has taken to promote workforce diversity and the challenges involved.

To address the testimony's objectives, GAO analyzed data from the Equal Employment Opportunity Commission (EEOC); reviewed select studies; and interviewed officials from financial services firms, trade organizations, and organizations that represent minority and women professionals. To the extent possible, key statistics have been updated.

Chapter 3 – During a hearing in 2004 on the financial services industry, congressional members and witnesses expressed concern about the industry's lack of workforce diversity, particularly in key management-level positions. Witnesses stated that financial services firms (e.g., banks and securities firms) had not made sufficient progress in recruiting and promoting minority and women candidates for management-level positions. Concerns were also raised about the ability of minority-owned businesses to raise capital (i.e., debt or equity capital).

GAO was asked to provide an overview on the status of diversity in the financial services industry. This report discusses (1) what available data show regarding diversity at the management level in the financial services industry from 1993 through 2004, (2) the types of initiatives that financial firms and related organizations have taken to promote workforce diversity and the challenges involved, and (3) the ability of minority- and women-owned businesses to obtain access to capital in financial markets and initiatives financial institutions have taken to make capital available to these businesses.

GAO makes no recommendations in this report.

In: Workforce Diversity in the Financial Sector   ISBN: 978-1-62808-442-9
Editors: E. Cruz and D. Houghton   © 2013 Nova Science Publishers, Inc.

Chapter 1

DIVERSITY MANAGEMENT: TRENDS AND PRACTICES IN THE FINANCIAL SERVICES INDUSTRY AND AGENCIES AFTER THE RECENT FINANCIAL CRISIS[*]

United States Government Accountability Office

WHY GAO DID THIS STUDY

As the U.S. workforce has become increasingly diverse, many private- and public-sector entities recognize the importance of recruiting and retaining minorities and women for management-level positions to improve their business. The 2007-2009 financial crisis has renewed questions about commitment within the financial services industry (e.g., banking and securities) to workforce diversity. The Dodd-Frank Act required that eight federal financial agencies and the Federal Reserve Banks implement provisions to support workforce and contractor diversity. GAO was asked to review trends and practices since the beginning of the financial crisis. This report examines (1) workforce diversity in the financial services industry, the federal financial agencies, and Reserve Banks, from 2007 through 2011 and (2) efforts of the agencies and Reserve Banks to implement workforce

---

[*] This is an edited, reformatted and augmented version of United States Government Accountability Office, Publication No. GAO-13-238, dated April 2013.

diversity practices under the Dodd-Frank Act, including contracting. GAO analyzed federal datasets and documents and interviewed industry representatives and officials from the federal financial agencies and Reserve Banks.

WHAT GAO RECOMMENDS

Each agency and Reserve Bank should include in its annual OMWI report to Congress efforts to measure the progress of its diversity practices. The agencies and Reserve Banks agreed to include this information in the annual OMWI reports. Additionally, some agencies and the Reserve Banks described steps they have taken or plan to take to address the recommendation.

WHAT GAO FOUND

Management-level representation of minorities and women in the financial services industry and among federal financial agencies and Federal Reserve Banks (Reserve Banks) has not changed substantially from 2007 through 2011. Industry representation of minorities in 2011 was higher in lower-level management positions—about 20 percent—compared to about 11 percent of senior-level manager positions. Industry representation of women at the overall management level remained at about 45 percent. Agency representation of minorities at the senior management level in 2011 ranged from 6 percent to 17 percent and from 0 percent to 44 percent at the Reserve Banks. Women's representation ranged from 31 to 47 percent at the agencies and from 15 to 58 percent at the Reserve Banks. Officials said the main challenge to improving diversity was identifying candidates, noting that minorities and women are often underrepresented in both internal and external candidate pools.

In response to the requirements in the Dodd-Frank Wall Street and Consumer Protection Act (Dodd-Frank Act), in 2011 federal financial agencies and Reserve Banks began to report annually on the recruitment and retention of minorities and women and other diversity practices. They all have established Offices of Minority and Women Inclusion (OMWI) as required. Many agencies and Reserve Banks indicated they had recruited from minority-serving institutions and partnered with organizations focused on developing opportunities for minorities and women, and most described plans to expand these activities. Some used employee surveys or recruiting metrics to measure the progress of their initiatives, as suggested by leading diversity practices, but OMWIs are not required to include this type of information in the annual reports to Congress. Better reporting of measurement efforts will provide Congress, agency officials, and other stakeholders additional insights on the effectiveness of diversity practices and demonstrate how agencies and Reserve Banks are following a leading diversity practice. Most federal financial agencies and Reserve Banks are in the early stages of implementing the contracting requirements required under the act. For example, most now include a provision in contracts for services requiring contractors to make efforts to ensure the fair inclusion of women and minorities in their workforce and subcontracted workforce and have established ways to evaluate compliance. The proportion of an agency's dollars awarded or a Reserve Bank's dollars paid to minority- or woman-owned businesses reported in 2011 OMWI reports ranged between 3 percent and 38 percent.

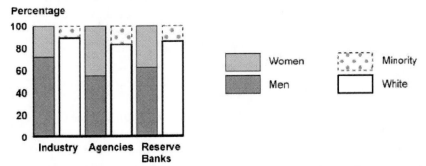

Source; GAO analysis of financial services industry EEOC data and agency and Reserve Bank reports.

Senior Management-Level Diversity, 2011.

ABBREVIATIONS

| AACSB | Association to Advance Collegiate Schools of Business |
| CFPB | Bureau of Consumer Financial Protection, known as the Consumer Financial Protection Bureau |

CPS	Current Population Survey
Dodd-Frank Act	Dodd–Frank Wall Street Reform and Consumer Protection Act
EEO	equal employment opportunity
EEO-1	Employer Information Report
EEOC	Equal Employment Opportunity Commission
FAR	Federal Acquisition Regulation
FDIC	Federal Deposit Insurance Corporation
Federal Reserve Board	Board of Governors of the Federal Reserve System
FHFA	Federal Housing Finance Agency
FSOC	Financial Stability Oversight Council
HERA	Housing and Economic Recovery Act of 2008
MWOB	minority- and women-owned business
MBA	Master of Business Administration
MD-715	EEOC Management Directive 715
NAICS	North American Industry Classification System
NCUA	National Credit Union Administration
NPO	National Procurement Office
OCC	Office of the Comptroller of the Currency
OMWI	Office of Minority and Women Inclusion
Reserve Banks	Federal Reserve Banks
SBA	Small Business Administration
SBS	security-based swap
SEC	Securities and Exchange Commission
Treasury	Departmental Offices of the Department of the Treasury

April 16, 2013

The Honorable Maxine Waters
Ranking Member
Committee on Financial Services
House of Representatives

Dear Ms. Waters:

As the U.S. workforce has become increasingly diverse, many private and public-sector organizations have recognized the importance of recruiting and retaining minorities and women for key positions to improve their business or organizational performance. Studies have associated a diversity of perspectives in organizations with innovation. However, congressional hearings have raised questions about diversity in the workforce of the financial services industry, which provides services that are essential to the continued growth and economic recovery of the country. During hearings on the financial services industry between 2004 and 2010, congressional members and witnesses expressed concern about the level of inclusion of women and minorities in the industry, particularly in key management-level positions.[1] The 2007-2009 financial crisis has renewed concerns about commitment within the financial services industry to workforce diversity and the number of federal contracting opportunities available to minority- and women-owned businesses. The Dodd-Frank Wall Street Reform and Consumer Protection Act (Dodd-Frank Act) included provisions requiring selected federal financial agencies and Federal Reserve Banks (Reserve Banks) each to establish an Office of Minority and Women Inclusion (OMWI).[2] The act required that these agencies and Reserve Banks establish the new diversity and inclusion offices to replace existing diversity programs by January 2011 and to begin addressing a number of other requirements in the act.[3]

This report updates our previous work by discussing changes in management-level diversity or diversity practices used in this industry since the beginning of the financial crisis in 2007. It also reviews the implementation of requirements in section 342 of the Dodd-Frank Act on workforce diversity. Specifically, our objectives were to discuss (1) what available data show about how the diversity of the financial services industry workforce and how diversity practices by the industry have changed from 2007 through 2011; (2) what available data show about how diversity in the workforces of the federal financial agencies and the Reserve Banks has changed from 2007 through 2011; (3) how these federal financial agencies and Reserve Banks are implementing workforce diversity practices under section 342 of the Dodd-Frank Act, including the extent to which their workforce diversity practices have changed since the financial crisis; and (4) the status of federal financial agencies' and Reserve Banks' implementation of the contracting provisions of the Dodd-Frank Act related to the inclusion of women and minorities.

To describe how diversity in the financial services industry and how the diversity practices it uses have changed from 2007 through 2011, we analyzed 2007-2011 workforce data from the Equal Employment Opportunity Commission's (EEOC) Employer Information Report (EEO-1) and from the Current Population Survey (CPS) produced by the Bureau of the Census and the Bureau of Labor Statistics. Through a review of documentation, electronic testing, and interviews with knowledgeable officials, we found these data sufficiently reliable for our use. We conducted a literature review to identify academic and industry studies on financial services workforce diversity, and we interviewed 10 industry representatives on these issues.

To review changes to the representation of women and minorities in the workforces of the agencies and Reserve Banks, we analyzed data the agencies submitted to EEOC from 2007 through 2011 in annual Equal Employment Opportunity Program Status Reports required by EEOC's MD-715 and analyzed EEO-1 reports provided by the 12 Reserve Banks.[4] We assessed the reliability of these data by conducting electronic testing, reviewing agency documentation, and interviewing agency officials. We determined that the data were sufficiently reliable for our use. We reviewed agency and Reserve Bank documentation of efforts to respond to the Dodd-Frank Act requirements, including annual OMWI reports to Congress. Additionally, we interviewed agency and Reserve Bank officials on changes in the inclusion of women and minorities in their workforces and any changes in the practices they used to further workforce diversity goals.

To determine the extent to which agencies and Reserve Banks are implementing the requirements of the Dodd-Frank Act regarding the inclusion of women and minorities in contracting, we reviewed annual OMWI reports submitted to Congress and interviewed officials on their efforts in this area. We collected and reviewed agency documentation of procedures developed to address the act's requirements, such as policy manuals, contract provisions related to promoting a diverse workforce, process workflows, and technical assistance materials.

We conducted this performance audit from January 2012 through April 2013 in accordance with generally accepted government auditing standards. Those standards require that we plan and perform the audit to obtain sufficient, appropriate evidence to provide a reasonable basis for our findings and conclusions based on our audit objectives. We believe that the evidence obtained provides a reasonable basis for our findings and conclusions based on our audit objectives.

BACKGROUND

The financial services industry is a major source of employment in the United States. EEOC data we obtained and analyzed showed that financial services firms we reviewed for this work employed more than 2.9 million people in 2011. We defined the financial services industry to include the following sectors:

- depository credit institutions, which include commercial banks, thrifts (savings and loan associations and savings banks), and credit unions;
- holdings and trusts, which include investment trusts, investment companies, and holding companies;
- nondepository credit institutions, which extend credit in the form of loans and include federally sponsored credit agencies, personal credit institutions, and mortgage bankers and brokers;
- the securities sector, which is composed of a variety of firms and organizations that bring together buyers and sellers of securities and commodities, manage investments, and offer financial advice; and
- the insurance sector, including carriers and insurance agents that provide protection against financial risks to policyholders in exchange for the payment of premiums.

Financial Services Industry and Diversity

We previously conducted work on the challenges faced in the financial sector for promoting and retaining a diverse workforce, focusing on private-sector firms.[5] In 2010, we reported that overall diversity at the management level in the financial services industry did not change substantially from 1993 through 2008 and that diversity in senior positions was limited. We also found that without a sustained commitment among financial services firms to overcoming challenges to recruiting and retaining minority candidates and obtaining "buy-in" from key employees, limited progress would be possible in fostering a more diverse workplace.

In a 2005 report, we defined diversity management as a process intended to create and maintain a positive work environment that values individuals' similarities and differences, so that all can reach their potential and maximize their contributions to an organization's strategic goals and objectives.[6] We also identified a set of nine leading diversity management practices that should be considered when an organization is developing and implementing diversity management. They are (1) commitment to diversity as demonstrated and communicated by an organization's top leadership; (2) the inclusion of diversity management in an organization's strategic plan; (3) diversity linked to performance, making the case that a more diverse and inclusive work environment could help improve productivity and individual and organizational performance; (4) measurement of the impact of various aspects of a diversity program; (5) management accountability for the progress of diversity initiatives; (6) succession planning; (7) recruitment; (8) employee involvement in an organization's diversity management; and (9) training for management and staff about diversity management.

Diversity Requirements under Section 342 of the Dodd-Frank Act

Section 342 of the Dodd-Frank Act required specific federal financial agencies and Reserve Banks each to establish, by January 21, 2011, an OMWI, responsible for matters relating to diversity in management, employment, and business activities.7 Table 1 describes the affected agencies.

The act's diversity provisions also apply to the Reserve Banks. The Federal Reserve System consists of a central governmental agency, the Board of Governors, in Washington, D.C., and 12 regional Reserve Banks. The 12 Reserve Banks are each responsible for a particular geographic area or district of the United States. They are located in Atlanta, Boston, Chicago, Cleveland, Dallas, Kansas City, Minneapolis, New York, Philadelphia, Richmond, San Francisco, and St. Louis. Unlike the Federal Reserve Board, the Reserve Banks are not federal agencies. Each Reserve Bank is a federally chartered corporation with a board of directors and member banks who are stockholders in the Reserve Bank. Under the Federal Reserve Act, Reserve Banks are subject to the general supervision of the Federal Reserve Board.[8]

The act's diversity provisions require the director of each OMWI to develop standards for (1) equal employment opportunity and the racial, ethnic and gender diversity of the workforce and senior management for the agency; (2) increased participation of minority- and women-owned businesses in the programs and contracts of the agency, including standards for coordinating technical assistance to such businesses; and (3) assessing the diversity policies and practices of entities regulated by the agency. It also provides that each

OMWI director advise his or her agency on the impact of agency policies and regulations on minority- and women-owned businesses.[9]

Table 1. Federal Financial Agencies Subject to Dodd-Frank Act Section 342

Agency	Function
Bureau of Consumer Financial Protection (CFPB)	Commonly known as the Consumer Financial Protection Bureau, writes rules to implement federal consumer financial law across banks and nonbanks; supervises for consumer protection purposes banks, thrifts, and credit unions with over $10 billion in assets and their affiliates, as well as nonbankmortgage-related firms, private student lenders, payday lenders, and certain other larger consumer financial companies; and enforces federal consumer financial law with respect to supervised entities and other nonbank entities.
Federal Deposit Insurance Corporation (FDIC)	Regulates FDIC-insured state-chartered banks that are not members of the Federal Reserve System, as well as federally insured state savings banks and thrifts; insures the deposits of all banks and thrifts that are approved for federal deposit insurance; and resolves all failed insured banks and thrifts and may resolve certain bank holding companies and nonbank financial companies.
Federal Housing Finance Agency (FHFA)	Supervises and regulates Fannie Mae, Freddie Mac, and the 12 Federal Home Loan Banks and their Office of Finance. Acts as conservator for Fannie Mae and Freddie Mac.
Board of Governors of the Federal Reserve System (Federal Reserve Board)	Regulates state-chartered banks that opt to be members of the Federal Reserve System, bank holding companies and certain subsidiaries, thrift holding companies, securities holding companies, Edge and agreement corporations, U.S. branches of foreign banks, any firm that is designated as systemically significant by the Financial Stability Oversight Council (FSOC), and payment, clearing, and settlement systems designated as systemically significant by FSOC, unless regulated by SEC or the Commodity Futures Trading Commission.
National Credit Union Administration (NCUA)	Charters and supervises federally chartered or insured credit unions and operates the National Credit Union Share Insurance Fund, which insures savings in federal and most state-chartered credit unions.
Office of the Comptroller of the Currency (OCC)	Charters and regulates national banks and federal thrifts and U.S. federal branches of foreign banks.
Securities and Exchange Commission (SEC)	Regulates securities exchanges, broker-dealers, investment companies, investment advisers, nationally recognized statistical rating organizations, security-based swap (SBS) dealers, major SBSparticipants, and SBS execution facilities.
Departmental Offices of the Department of the Treasury (Treasury)	The Department of the Treasury is organized into two major components: the departmental offices and the operating bureaus. The departmental offices are primarily responsible for the formulation of policy and management of the department as a whole, and include domestic finance, economic policy, international affairs, and others.

Source: GAO review of agency documentation.

The act also outlines steps the specific agencies and Reserve Banks should take to seek workforce diversity at all levels of their organizations. Among other things, these steps include recruiting from colleges serving primarily minority populations, sponsoring and recruiting at job fairs in urban communities, and advertising positions in newspapers and magazines oriented toward minorities and women.

In addition, the act provides that each OMWI director develop and implement standards and procedures to ensure, to the maximum extent possible, the fair inclusion and utilization of minorities, women, and minority- and women-owned businesses in all business and activities of the agency at all levels, including in procurement, insurance, and all types of contracts. Agency procedures for reviewing and evaluating applicable contract proposals and for hiring service providers should include a component that gives consideration to applicant diversity, to the extent consistent with applicable laws.[10] Additionally, the act mandates that the OMWI director develop procedures to determine whether contractors, or subcontractors when applicable, have made a good faith effort to include minorities and women in their workforces. It requires that each OMWI director recommend that contracts be terminated if they determine that an agency contractor, and as applicable, a subcontractor has failed to make a good faith effort to include minorities and women in their workforce.

Upon receipt of such a recommendation, the head of an agency may terminate the contract, make a referral to an office in the Department of Labor, or take other appropriate action.

Finally, the act requires each OMWI to submit to Congress an annual report detailing the actions taken by the agency and the OMWI to comply with the provisions in section 342.

The annual reports are required to include, among other things, annual amounts paid to contractors, including the percentage of the amounts that were paid to minorities, women, and minority- and women-owned businesses; any challenges in contracting with qualified minority- and women-owned businesses; any challenges in hiring qualified minority and women employees; and any other information, findings, conclusions, and recommendations for legislative or agency action as the OMWI director determines appropriate.

INDUSTRY DIVERSITY LEVELS REMAINED ABOUT THE SAME FROM 2007 THROUGH 2011

Diversity has remained about the same at the management level in terms of the representation of both minorities and women, while industry representatives noted the continued use of leading diversity practices and some challenges. According to EEOC data, the representation of minorities at the management level stood at 19 percent in 2011. The representation of women in management remained at about 45 percent, according to EEOC data. The nine leading diversity practices that we previously identified in 2005 remain relevant today, according to industry representatives with whom we spoke. Industry representatives also noted some challenges, such as the difficulty in recruitment because of a limited supply of diverse candidates.

Diversity in the Financial Services Industry Remained about the Same at the Management Level from 2007 through 2011

At the overall management level, the representation of minorities increased from 17.3 percent to 19 percent from 2007 through 2011 according to EEOC data we obtained, which are reported by financial services firms (see fig. 1).[11] While this is not a substantial increase, it shows a continued upward trend from our 2006 report, in which data showed that management-level representation by minorities increased from 11.1 percent to 15.5 percent from 1993 through 2004.[12]

The representation of minorities varied among management positions, which EEOC splits into two categories: (1) first- and mid-level officials and managers and (2) senior-level officials and managers. In 2011, the representation of minorities among first- and mid-level managers stood at 20.4 percent, about 1 percentage point higher to the representation of minorities among all management positions, according to EEOC data (see fig. 2). In contrast, at the senior management level, representation of minorities was 10.8 percent in 2011, about 8 percentage points below their representation among all management positions; yet representation of minorities in first- and mid-level management positions consistently increased from 18.7 percent to 20.4 percent over the 5-year period. First- and mid-level management positions may serve as an internal pipeline in an organization through which minority candidates could move into senior management positions.

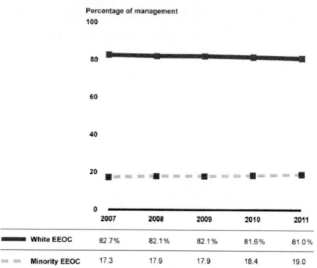

	2007	2008	2009	2010	2011
White EEOC	82.7%	82.1%	82.1%	81.6%	81.0%
Minority EEOC	17.3	17.9	17.9	18.4	19.0

Source: GAO analysis of EEOC data.

Figure 1. Percentage of White and Minority Managers in the Financial Services Industry, 2007-2011.

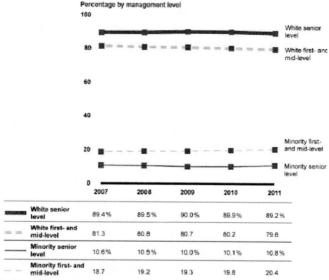

	2007	2008	2009	2010	2011
White senior level	89.4%	89.5%	90.0%	89.9%	89.2%
White first- and mid-level	81.3	80.8	80.7	80.2	79.6
Minority senior level	10.6%	10.5%	10.0%	10.1%	10.8%
Minority first- and mid-level	18.7	19.2	19.3	19.8	20.4

Source: GAO analysis of EEOC data.

Figure 2. Percentage of Whites and Minorities in First- and Mid-Level Management and Senior Management Positions in the Financial Services Industry, 2007-2011.

Similar to the total representation of minorities across all management positions, specific races/ethnicities have not changed significantly, but EEOC data show slight variations of representation for specific races/ethnicities. For example, the representation of African Americans decreased from 6.5 percent in 2007 to 6.3 percent in 2011, according to EEOC data (see fig. 3). In contrast, representation of most other races/ethnicities increased, and the highest increase was in the representation of Asians, from 5.4 percent to 6.5 percent over the same time period.

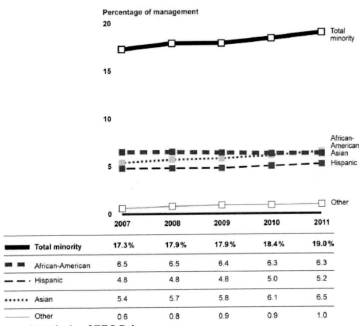

	2007	2008	2009	2010	2011
Total minority	17.3%	17.9%	17.9%	18.4%	19.0%
African-American	6.5	6.5	6.4	6.3	6.3
Hispanic	4.8	4.8	4.8	5.0	5.2
Asian	5.4	5.7	5.8	6.1	6.5
Other	0.6	0.8	0.9	0.9	1.0

Source: GAO analysis of EEOC data.

Figure 3. Percentage of Specific Races/Ethnicities in the Financial Services Industry in Overall Management Positions, 2007-2011.

From 2007 to 2011, the representation of African Americans went down in both management levels, while the representation of other specific races/ethnicities either increased or remained stable (see fig. 4). At the senior management level, the representation of Asians remained stable at about 4.1 percent from 2007 through 2011. However, the representation of African Americans in senior management positions decreased from 3.1 percent to 2.7 percent, and the representation of Hispanics increased from 3 percent to 3.3

percent. Among first- and mid-level management positions, the representation of Asians increased from 5.6 percent to 6.9 percent and the representation of Hispanics increased from 5.2 percent to 5.5 percent, while the representation of African Americans decreased from 7.2 percent to 6.9 percent.

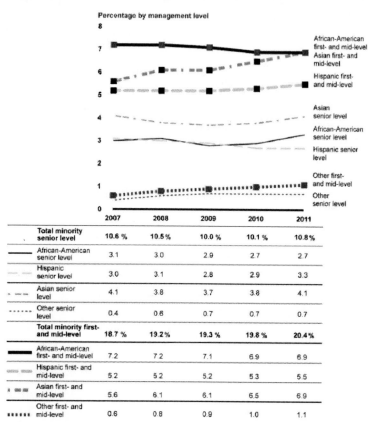

Source: GAO analysis of EEOC data.

	2007	2008	2009	2010	2011
Total minority senior level	10.6 %	10.5%	10.0 %	10.1 %	10.8%
African-American senior level	3.1	3.0	2.9	2.7	2.7
Hispanic senior level	3.0	3.1	2.8	2.9	3.3
Asian senior level	4.1	3.8	3.7	3.8	4.1
Other senior level	0.4	0.6	0.7	0.7	0.7
Total minority first- and mid-level	18.7 %	19.2%	19.3 %	19.8 %	20.4%
African-American first- and mid-level	7.2	7.2	7.1	6.9	6.9
Hispanic first- and mid-level	5.2	5.2	5.2	5.3	5.5
Asian first- and mid-level	5.6	6.1	6.1	6.5	6.9
Other first- and mid-level	0.6	0.8	0.9	1.0	1.1

Figure 4. Percentage of Specific Races/Ethnicities in the Financial Services Industry at Various Management Levels, 2007-2011.

Over the same 5-year period, the representation of women at the management level remained at about 45 percent in EEOC data, which show a slight decrease from 45.1 percent to 44.7 percent (see fig. 5). In 2006, we reported an increase with representation of women at about 42.9 percent in 1993 to about 45.8 percent in 2004.[13]

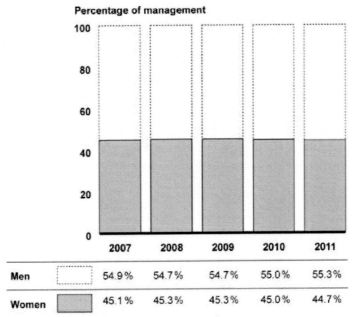

Source: GAO analysis of EEOC data.

Figure 5. Percentage of Men and Women in Management Positions in the Financial
Services Industry, 2007-2011.

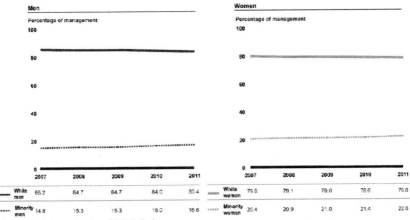

Source: GAO analysis of EEOC data.

Figure 6. Percentage of White and Minority Men and White and Minority Women in
Management Positions in the Financial Services Industry, 2007-2011.

Among all women in management positions, EEOC data showed that the representation of minority women increased, from 20.4 percent to 22 percent over the same 5-year period (see fig. 6). In addition, EEOC data show that the representation of minority men increased from 14.8 percent to 16.6 percent.

Among first- and mid-level management positions, the representation of women has been at about 48 percent, slightly higher than the representation of women among all management positions. In contrast, women represented about 29 percent of all senior management positions from 2007 through 2011—about 16 percentage points below the representation of women for all management positions, according to EEOC data (see fig. 7).

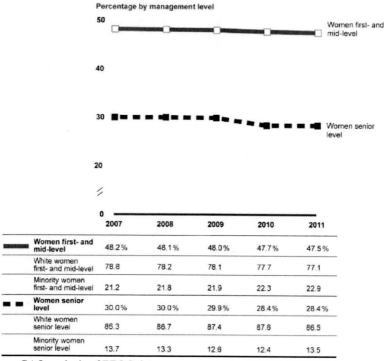

		2007	2008	2009	2010	2011
	Women first- and mid-level	48.2%	48.1%	48.0%	47.7%	47.5%
	White women first- and mid-level	78.8	78.2	78.1	77.7	77.1
	Minority women first- and mid-level	21.2	21.8	21.9	22.3	22.9
	Women senior level	30.0%	30.0%	29.9%	28.4%	28.4%
	White women senior level	86.3	86.7	87.4	87.6	86.5
	Minority women senior level	13.7	13.3	12.6	12.4	13.5

Source: GAO analysis of EEOC data.

Figure 7. Percentage of Women in the Financial Services Industry by Management Level and Race/Ethnicity, 2007-2011.

Based on EEOC data, minority women had greater representation at the first and mid levels of management compared to the senior level over the 5-year period. As shown in figure 7, among female senior managers, representation of minority women remained at about 13 percent over the 5-year period. In contrast, among female first- and mid-level managers, the proportion of minority women increased during the same period from 21.2 percent to 22.9 percent.

The representation of minorities increases for both women and men as the firm size increases (see fig. 8). For example, in 2011 the representation of minorities at firms with 100-249 employees was about 18 percent among women and about 12 percent among men, while at firms with more than 1,000 employees, the representation of minorities was about 23 percent among women and about 17 percent among men. For additional analysis of EEOC data by workforce position and industry sector, see appendix II.

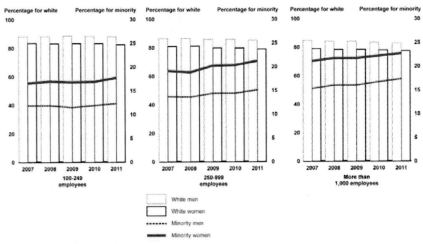

Source: GAO analysis of EEOC data.

Figure 8. Percentage of Whites/Minorities and Men/Women at Financial Services Firms of Different Sizes, 2007-2011.

A survey of the general population shows some similar trends in the representation of both women and minorities in the financial services industry. The CPS is administered by the Bureau of the Census for the Bureau of Labor Statistics and is a monthly survey of about 60,000 households across the nation. The CPS is used to produce official government figures on total employment and unemployment issued each month. According to the CPS data, from 2007 through 2011 the representation of women at the management level decreased from an estimated 49.1 percent to 47.3 percent. In addition, CPS data show a smaller increase from an estimated 14.1 percent to 15.1

percent in the representation of minorities in management over the same 5-year period.[14]

Leading Diversity Practices Remain Relevant but Challenges Exist Regarding Recruitment and Other Issues

The nine leading diversity practices that we previously identified in 2005 are still relevant today, according to industry representatives with whom we spoke.[15] Some industry representatives highlighted practices among these nine that they considered the most important to foster diversity and inclusion in their organizations. For example, top leadership commitment drives the other eight leading diversity practices, according to 9 of 10 industry representatives. In addition, accountability helps to promote the implementation of the other leading diversity practices because an issue is more likely to be addressed if it is tracked, according to 2 industry representatives. Moreover, creating awareness of the benefits of diversity for an organization among management and employees is important because it increases commitment to further the diversity goals of the organization, according to 7 industry representatives whom we interviewed.[16] However, 1 industry representative told us there are still some firms that do not see the importance of diversity. In addition, 2 industry representatives said these 9 leading diversity practices should be expanded beyond workforce management to include, for example, an organization's contracting efforts.

Some industry representatives also noted that measuring the impact of various diversity practices is an important practice but that it can also be challenging; for example, it can be difficult to link specific practices to diversity outcomes and it can be a long-term process. According to some industry representatives, financial services organizations may measure the effectiveness of their diversity practices by assessing attrition, recruiting, and promotion rates, which are similar to measures we had previously reported.[17] For example, a financial services organization may measure the proportion of certain minority groups or women in its workforce or among its promotions to determine the effectiveness of its practices. Further, financial services firms may use surveys to gather employee perspectives on workforce diversity issues in the organization, such as perceived fairness in the promotion process or factors that affect an employee's decision to remain with the firm, among other topics.

Additional diversity practices identified by some industry representatives that can support the leading diversity practices include the following:

- *Sponsor individuals.* Sponsorship of women within an organization where an executive acts as a guide to help women navigate the organization and expand their networks is an important diversity practice, according to three industry representatives. This sponsorship practice goes beyond the mentoring programs we previously reported in 2006, as a sponsor acts as an advocate to help the individual advance within the organization.[18]
- *Address biased perceptions.* One industry representative told us about an effort to combat unconscious bias in promotions. They described a promotion system designed to address biased perceptions, such as a view of leaders as being typically male. According to the industry representative, the firm that employed this diversity practice gathered complete and objective evaluations of employees and trained its managers to recognize and address these perceptions. The result was that the firm promoted greater numbers of women into management.

No industry representatives that we contacted reported changes to diversity practices as a result of the challenges faced by many firms during the financial crisis. Although representation of minorities and women has remained about the same from 2007 through 2011, according to some industry representatives, the industry continues to be focused on diversity. However, three industry representatives did cite specific instances where funding was scaled back as a result of the recent financial crisis. One industry representative told us that investment in training programs was reduced across the organization, but when a measureable impact on employees was identified at this organization, steps were taken to address the impact.

Some industry representatives cited challenges to achieving a diverse workforce in general. We have previously reported some of these challenges, which can affect some of the leading diversity practices.[19] Six industry representatives said that diversity recruitment is difficult because the supply (or "pipeline") of minority and women candidates is limited. This has been a consistent challenge that we previously reported in 2006 and 2010.[20] Available data indicate that for the internal pool of potential candidates for some management positions, representation of women varied, while representation of minorities was higher in every nonmanagement category compared to management positions (see fig. 9).

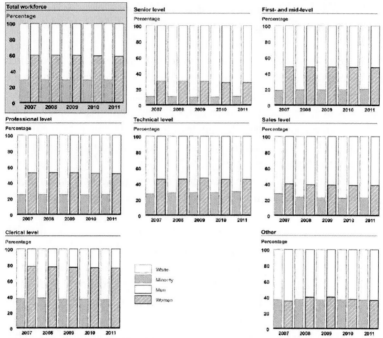

Source: GAO analysis of EEOC data.

Note: The following are descriptions of the job categories in EEO-1 data from EEOC: (1) "Executive/Senior Level Officials and Managers," includes individuals who reside in the highest levels of organizations and plan, direct, and formulate policies, set strategy, and provide the overall direction of enterprises/organizations for the development and delivery of products or services, within the parameters approved by boards of directors or other governing bodies; (2) "First/Mid-Level Officials and Managers," includes individuals who receive directions from Executive/Senior Level management, and oversee and direct the delivery of products, services, or functions at group, regional, or divisional levels of organizations; (3) "professionals" include occupations requiring either college graduation or experience of such kind and amount as to provide a comparable background; (4) "technicians" include occupations requiring a combination of basic scientific knowledge and manual skill that can be obtained through 2 years of post-high school education; (5) "sales workers" include occupations engaging wholly or primarily in direct selling; (6) "office and clerical" includes all clerical-type work regardless of level of difficulty, where the activities are predominantly nonmanual; and (7) the category "other" includes craft workers, operatives, laborers, and service workers.

Figure 9. Percentage of Whites/Minorities and Men/Women in Various Financial Services Industry Workforce Positions, 2007- 2011.

For example, in 2011 the representation of women was greater in professional positions (about 51 percent) compared to sales positions (about 38 percent). In addition, the representation of minorities was higher in all nonmanagement positions than at the management level in 2011, but especially higher in technical and clerical positions at more than 29 percent in both types of positions. Further analysis of diversity in various workforce positions can be found in appendix II.

Table 2. Percentage of Students Enrolled in MBA Degree Programs at AACSB Member Schools in the United States by Race/Ethnicity, 2007-2011

Year	Total enrolled	White	Total minority	African American	Hispanic	Asian	Other
2007	100%	74%	26%	7%	6%	12%	0%
2008	100	73	27	8	6	12	0
2009	100	73	27	8	7	12	0
2010	100	72	28	9	7	11	1
2011	100	71	29	9	7	11	2

Source: GAO analysis of AACSB International data.

Note: The "other" category includes Native American, and updated race/ethnicity categories implemented in 2011 to include "two or more races" and "Native Hawaiian or Other Pacific Islander." Percentages may not always add exactly due to rounding. In addition, these ratios only represent MBA enrolled students for whom race/ethnicity was indicated.

In recent years, representation in business graduate programs, a potential source of future managers in the financial industry, has remained stable for women and has increased slightly for minorities, but representation is still low for both women and minorities when compared to the overall representation of students in the university system.[21] To assess one possible external pool of candidates for financial services firms, we obtained data from the Association to Advance Collegiate Schools of Business (AACSB) on the number of students enrolled in Master of Business Administration (MBA) degree programs in AACSB member schools in the United States from 2007 through 2011 as well as the number of students in the university system.[22] According to AACSB data, the representation of women remained constant over this period, while the representation of minorities increased. For example, the representation of women among MBA students remained at about 37 percent over the 5-year period, while representation of women was slightly higher in the overall university system at about 41 percent. In contrast, as table 2 shows, the representation of minorities increased among MBA students from about 26 percent in 2007 to about 29 percent in 2011. However, when compared to the university system, representation of minorities in the overall university system was slightly higher from about 29 percent in 2007 to 34 percent in 2011.

Some industry representatives stated that the negative perception of the industry could also limit the external pipeline of potential candidates, which can make recruitment challenging. Multiple industry representatives discussed the need to take a new approach to diversity recruiting as a result of the negative image many potential candidates may have about the financial services industry following the recent financial crisis. For example, to counter negative perceptions that may have resulted from the foreclosure crisis or the Occupy Wall Street movement, one industry representative told us that it explains to prospective employees the social contributions financial services firms make through microfinance or economic and community development.

In addition to these difficulties with recruiting, two industry representatives highlighted maintaining accountability as a particular challenge for financial services firms.[23] For example, an industry representative said it is difficult to promote results in diversity by linking diversity management with managers' performance ratings because this practice may not provide enough incentive to many managers. Another industry representative told us that recognizing and compensating managers and employees for their diversity efforts can result in increased commitment to foster workforce diversity and an increase in diversity at firms.

AGENCY AND RESERVE BANK WORKFORCE DIVERSITY VARIED, AND OFFICIALS REPORTED DIFFICULTY IDENTIFYING DIVERSE CANDIDATES

Since the financial crisis, senior management-level minority and gender diversity at the federal financial agencies and Reserve Banks has varied across individual entities.[24] The representation of minorities at the senior management-level increased slightly overall at both the agencies and Reserve Banks. In addition, the representation of women at the senior management-level increased slightly overall for both the agencies and Reserve Banks. Agency and Reserve Bank officials identified key challenges to increasing workforce diversity overall and at the senior management-level, including limited representation of minorities and women among internal and external candidate pools.

Senior Management-Level Representation of Minorities and Women Varied at Agencies and Reserve Banks, with Slight Changes Overall

Senior management-level representation of minorities and women varied across individual federal financial agencies and the 12 Reserve Banks. The agencies included FDIC, the Federal Reserve Board, NCUA, OCC, and Treasury. Complete data for this period were not available for CFPB, FHFA, and SEC, and we excluded these agencies from our analysis of changes in senior management-level diversity from 2007 through 2011, but provide recent data when available. Data for each agency are provided in appendix IV. CFPB assumed responsibility for certain consumer financial protection functions in July 2011 and has not yet reported workforce information to EEOC.[25] However, we received recent employment profile data from CFPB as of May 2012.[26] FHFA, which was established in July 2008, started reporting workforce data for 2010; while our analysis provides 2010 and 2011 data for FHFA, our analysis across the agencies excludes FHFA from aggregated totals. SEC reported data for 2007 through 2011, but revised how it reported officials and managers during the 5-year period; while our analysis provides 2011 senior management-level data for SEC, we excluded SEC from our senior management-level trend analysis.

In our review of agency reports, we found that from 2007 through 2011, the representation of minorities among senior management-level employees, when aggregated across FDIC, the Federal Reserve Board, NCUA, OCC, and Treasury, increased slightly, from 16 to 17 percent for the agencies combined (see fig. 10).[27] From 2007 through 2011, three agencies—FDIC, the Federal Reserve Board, and Treasury—showed an increase in the representation of minorities at the senior management-level, by between 1 and 3 percentage points. Two agencies—NCUA and OCC—experienced no percentage point change in their representation of minorities at the senior management-level from 2007 through 2011.[28] In 2011, the representation of minorities among senior management-level employees of these agencies, FHFA, and SEC ranged from 11 percent at SEC to 24 percent at FHFA. Additionally, CFPB employment data showed about 28 percent representation of minorities among senior officials as of May 2012.[29]

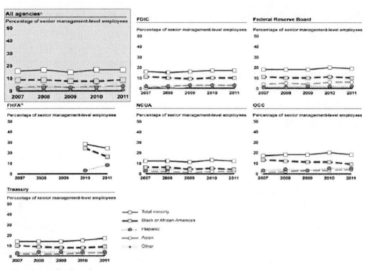

Source: GAO analysis of agency reports.

Notes: Percentages are rounded to the nearest percent.

For our analysis, we reviewed the numbers of employees the agencies reported according to race/ethnicity and gender in table A3 of their MD-715 reports from 2007 through 2011. These data are based on information self-reported by employees to each agency and there were some differences in reporting across the agencies. In some years, some agencies reported all employees— permanent and temporary—in their A3 tables while others reported permanent employees only. We considered employees reported by agencies in the category "Executive/Senior Level" as senior management-level employees. Though the MD-715 report guidelines instruct agencies to identify employees Grades 15 and above who have supervisory responsibility in this category, agencies have discretion to include employees who have significant policymaking responsibilities but do not supervise employees. As a result, the composition of the "Executive/Senior Level" category may vary among the different agencies and does not necessarily involve the same set of managers at each agency.

[a] Our trend analysis for "all agencies" excludes CFPB, FHFA, and SEC. CFPB assumed responsibility for certain consumer financial protection functions in July 2011 and has not yet reported workforce information to EEOC. FHFA was established in 2008 and started reporting workforce data for 2010. SEC revised how it reported officials and managers between 2007 and 2011. While our analysis includes 2011 management-level data for SEC, we excluded SEC from our trend analysis.

For more information on the graphs see Table 7 in Appendix IV.

Figure 10. Percentage of Minorities among Senior Management-Level Employees at Six Federal Financial Agencies, 2007- 2011.

In our review of EEO-1 reports provided by the Reserve Banks, we found that the representation of minorities among senior management-level employees in aggregate across the 12 Reserve Banks increased from 11 percent to 14 percent from 2007 through 2011 (see fig.11).[30] The population of senior management-level employees at each bank in 2011 ranged from 9 employees at the Reserve Banks of Chicago, Dallas, and Minneapolis, to 59 employees at the Reserve Bank of New York, and the population of minority senior management-level employees at each bank ranged from zero employees at the Reserve Bank of Cleveland to 7 employees at the Reserve Bank of New York. Specific information on each Reserve Bank is provided in appendix IV.

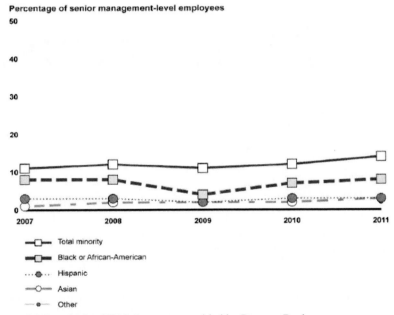

Source: GAO analysis of EEO-1 reports provided by Reserve Banks.

Notes: Data are rounded to the nearest percent.

Reserve Bank data are presented in aggregate because the population of senior management-level employees at most Reserve Banks is generally small and the gain or loss of one employee can result in a large percentage point change in the representation of minorities. Specific information on each Reserve Bank is provided in appendix IV.

For more information on the graph see Table 8 in Appendix IV.

Figure 11. Percentage of Minorities among Senior Management-Level Employees at the 12 Reserve Banks, 2007-2011.

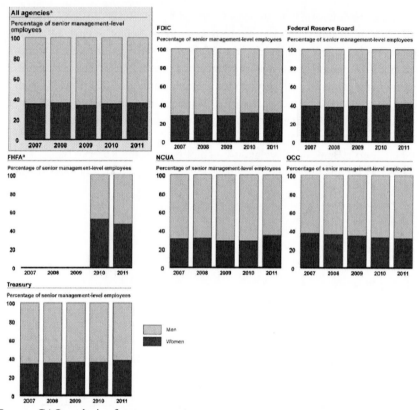

Source: GAO analysis of agency reports.

Notes: Percentages are rounded to the nearest percent.

For our analysis, we reviewed the numbers of employees the agencies reported according to race/ethnicity and gender in table A3 of their MD-715 reports from 2007 through 2011. These data are based on information self-reported by employees to each agency and there were some differences in reporting across the agencies. In some years, some agencies reported all employees— permanent and temporary—in their A3 tables while others reported permanent employees only. We considered employees reported by agencies in the category "Executive/Senior Level" as senior management-level employees. Though the MD-715 report guidelines instruct agencies to identify employees Grades 15 and above who have supervisory responsibility in this category, agencies have discretion to include employees who have significant policymaking responsibilities but do not supervise employees. As a result, the composition of the "Executive/Senior Level" category may vary among the different agencies and does not necessarily involve the same set of managers at each agency.

[a]Our trend analysis for "all agencies" excludes CFPB, FHFA, and SEC. CFPB
    assumed responsibility for certain consumer financial protection functions in July
    2011 and has not yet reported workforce information to EEOC. FHFA was
    established in 2008 and started reporting workforce data for 2010. SEC revised
    how it reported officials and managers between 2007 and 2011. While our
    analysis includes 2011 management-level data for SEC, we excluded SEC from
    our trend analysis.
For more information on the graphs see Table 9 in Appendix IV.

Figure 12. Percentage of Women among Senior Management-Level Employees at Six
Federal Financial Agencies, 2007-2011.

In general, the representation of women at the senior management-level
increased slightly since the beginning of the financial crisis in 2007 at
agencies, but representation percentages varied for each entity. In our review
of agency reports, we found that from 2007 through 2011, the representation
of women at the senior management-level increased slightly from 34 to 36
percent across FDIC, the Federal Reserve Board, NCUA, OCC, and Treasury,
in aggregate (see fig. 12). Changes varied by agency, from a decrease of 5
percentage points at OCC to an increase of 5 percentage points at NCUA. Four
of the five agencies—FDIC, the Federal Reserve Board, NCUA, and
Treasury—showed an increase of between 3 and 5 percentage points in the
representation of women at the senior management-level from 2007 through
2011. In 2011, the representation of women among senior management-level
employees ranged among the agencies from 31 percent at FDIC to 47 percent
at FHFA. Additionally, CFPB employment data showed the representation of
women among senior officials at about 35 percent as of May 2012.

In our review of EEO-1 reports provided by the Reserve Banks, we found
that from 2007 through 2011, the representation of women at the senior
management-level increased from 32 percent to 38 percent for the Reserve
Banks, in aggregate (see fig. 13). As mentioned previously, the population of
senior management-level employees at each bank in 2011 ranged from nine
employees at the Reserve Banks of Chicago, Dallas, and Minneapolis, to 59
employees at the Reserve Bank of New York. The population of women
among senior management-level employees at each bank in 2011 ranged from
two employees at the Reserve Bank of Boston to 25 employees at the Reserve
Bank of New York. Specific information on each Reserve Bank is provided in
appendix IV.

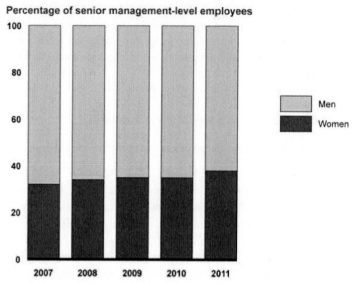

Source: GAO analysis of Reserve Bank reports.

Notes: Data are rounded to the nearest percent.

Reserve Bank data are presented in aggregate because the population of senior management-level employees at most Reserve Banks is generally small and the gain or loss of one employee can result in a large percentage point change in the representation of women. Specific information on each Reserve Bank is provided in appendix IV.

For more information on the graph see Table 10 in Appendix IV.

Figure 13. Percentage of Women among Senior Management-Level Employees at the 12 Reserve Banks, 2007-2011.

Several agencies reported on existing diversity practices related to retaining and promoting employees to build management-level diversity. For example, according to agency reports, some Treasury offices conduct formal mentoring programs, and the Federal Reserve Board has customized mentoring programs within its divisions, which in conjunction with a leadership exchange program sponsored by the Federal Reserve System, provide employees opportunities to develop new skills and experiences. Further, OCC reported having development programs for employees within its bank supervision division that provide leadership and development opportunities to staff, and agency-sponsored employee network groups implemented mentoring circles to assist in the career development and retention of the agency's workforce.

Several Reserve Banks identified practices targeted to improve management-level diversity, including changes to hiring practices and mentoring programs. For example, officials from several Reserve Banks we contacted said their organizations revised their hiring policies to open all management-level positions to external applicants in addition to current employees as a way to build management-level diversity by hiring diverse, experienced candidates from outside the organization. Additionally, the Reserve Banks of Dallas and New York began piloting new mentoring programs in 2011, and each planned to expand its program based on initial feedback its OMWI had received. These banks and several others with existing mentoring programs reported that mentoring programs were important to retaining and developing minorities and women within their organizations. Later in this report, we provide additional information on the agencies' and Reserve Banks' recruitment practices as part of their efforts to implement section 342 of the Dodd-Frank Act.[31]

Total Workforce Minorities and Women Representation Varied but Decreased Slightly Overall

Based on our analysis of minority and gender diversity at all levels from 2007 through 2011, workforce diversity varied at the federal financial agencies and Reserve Banks, with slight decreases in aggregate. Specifically, the representation of minorities decreased slightly from 31 percent to 30 percent from 2007 through 2011 across FDIC, the Federal Reserve Board, NCUA, OCC, SEC, and Treasury, in aggregate. Additionally, CFPB employment data showed the representation of minorities of all agency employees at about 33 percent as of May 2012. Three agencies—NCUA, OCC, and SEC—showed a 1 percentage point or greater increase in the overall representation of minorities during the 5- year period, according to agency reports. In 2011, the representation of minorities at the agencies ranged from 25 percent at NCUA to 44 percent at the Federal Reserve Board. Our analysis of EEO-1 reports provided by the Reserve Banks for 2007 through 2011 showed that the representation of minorities across the Reserve Banks declined slightly in aggregate, from 38 percent to 36 percent. The Reserve Banks of Minneapolis and New York showed a 2 percentage point increase in the overall representation of minorities working at Reserve Banks, the Reserve Bank of Boston showed no percentage point change, and the remaining nine banks showed decreases of 1 to 8 percentage points. In 2011, the representation of minorities at the Reserve Banks ranged from 16 percent at the Reserve Bank of Kansas City to 53 percent at the Reserve Bank of San Francisco.

Similarly, we found that overall gender diversity varied at individual agencies and Reserve Banks, and generally declined slightly from 2007 through 2011. The overall representation of women in the workforce aggregated across FDIC, the Federal Reserve Board, NCUA, OCC, SEC, and Treasury declined slightly from 47 percent to 45 percent over the 5- year period. Additionally, CFPB employment data showed the representation of women of all agency employees at about 49 percent as of May 2012. Two agencies—NCUA and SEC—showed no percentage point change in the representation of women during the 5-year period; OCC showed a decrease of about 1 percentage point, and the other three agencies—FDIC, the Federal Reserve Board, and Treasury— experienced decreases of 2 percentage points. In 2011, the representation of women among all employees at the agencies ranged from 42 percent at FDIC to 48 percent at SEC and Treasury. The overall representation of women across the Reserve Banks, in aggregate, declined from 49 percent to 45 percent from 2007 through 2011. All Reserve Banks showed declines in the representation of women among all employees during the 5-year period, ranging from a 1 percentage point decrease at the Reserve Bank of New York to a 7 percentage point decrease at the Reserve Bank of Cleveland. For example, in 2007, 827 of the Reserve Bank of Cleveland's 1,568 employees were women, and in 2011, 500 of the bank's 1,094 employees were women; the bank's workforce changed from having around 53 percent women employees to about 46 percent women employees. In 2011, the overall representation of women at Reserve Banks ranged from 40 percent at the Reserve Banks of Philadelphia and Richmond to 53 percent at the Reserve Bank of Minneapolis. See appendix III for additional information on the overall workforce representation for the agencies and Reserve Banks.

According to officials from five Reserve Banks and the Federal Reserve Board, consolidation of check processing and other operations, some of which occurred since the financial crisis, had eliminated many administrative and service worker positions. Since these positions are often held by minorities and women, these consolidations affected overall employment diversity at affected Reserve Banks. In response to declines in the use of paper checks and greater use of electronic payments, the Reserve Banks took steps beginning in 2003 to reduce the number of locations where paper checks were processed. In 2001, the Federal Reserve System employed around 5,500 people in check processing functions across 45 locations, and in 2008, around 2,800 employees supported check processing functions across 18 locations. By 2010, one paper check processing site remained in Cleveland, along with an electronic check processing site in Atlanta. As of January 2013, approximately 480 employees supported check processing functions across the Federal Reserve System. The Federal Reserve System is projected to complete its consolidation of check processing functions in 2013.

Officials Reported Difficulty Identifying Diverse Candidates as the Main Challenge to Building Workforce Diversity

OMWI officials described challenges to building workforce diversity both at the management level and overall. Four agencies—FDIC, the Federal Reserve Board, FHFA, and OCC—and three Reserve Banks—the Reserve Banks of Chicago, Minneapolis, and St. Louis—cited underrepresentation of minorities and women within internal candidate pools as a challenge to building management-level diversity, as many management-level positions are filled through promotions or internal hiring processes. Additionally, the Reserve Banks of Dallas, Minneapolis, Philadelphia, and San Francisco said low turnover was a challenge to increasing their management-level diversity profiles because it limited opportunities to increase organizational diversity through hiring and promotion.

Federal financial agencies and Reserve Banks identified other challenges to building workforce diversity generally. The Reserve Banks of Atlanta, Boston, Chicago, Kansas City, and St. Louis cited competition from the private sector for recruiting diverse candidates as a challenge. In addition, FHFA and the Reserve Banks of Cleveland, Philadelphia, and San Francisco cited limited representation of minorities within external candidate pools as another challenge. The Federal Reserve Board and the Reserve Banks of Chicago and Kansas City reported that the availability of external candidates could be an issue in particular for hiring certain specialized positions, such as economists, which would involve a small candidate pool with limited representation of minorities. Additionally, three Reserve Banks identified geographic impediments to their national recruitment efforts, explaining that it is difficult to attract candidates from outside their region. For example, the Reserve Banks of Kansas City and St. Louis said it was difficult to recruit candidates lacking ties to the central United States, and the Reserve Bank of San Francisco cited difficulty recruiting from the eastern United States. Further, several agencies and Reserve Banks identified other challenges to building workforce diversity. For example, Treasury cited budget constraints on hiring and the Reserve Bank of Cleveland cited time constraints on recruitment practices as challenges. Additionally, NCUA cited as a challenge establishing tracking systems to help identify barriers to recruiting, hiring, and retaining minorities.

DODD-FRANK REQUIREMENTS ARE BEING IMPLEMENTED, BUT ENHANCED REPORTING OF EFFORTS TO MEASURE PROGRESS IS NEEDED

Federal financial agencies and Reserve Banks have begun implementing key requirements of section 342 of the Dodd-Frank Act. First, all agencies and Reserve Banks have established OMWIs. Most agencies and all of the Reserve Banks used existing policies to establish standards for equal employment opportunity required by the act. Although many agencies and Reserve Banks had been using recruitment practices required by the act prior to its enactment, the majority of OMWIs have expanded these or initiated other practices. In addition to meeting requirements regarding their diversity policies, the federal financial agencies have taken preliminary steps to develop procedures for assessing the diversity policies and practices of entities they regulate, as required under the act. Finally, nearly all the agencies and all of the Reserve Banks are reporting annually on their diversity practices. While many OMWIs have implemented or are planning efforts to measure and evaluate the progress of their diversity and inclusion activities, information on such efforts is not yet reported consistently across the OMWI annual reports. Such information could enhance their efforts to report on measuring outcomes and the progress of their diversity practices.

Agencies and Reserve Banks Have Established Offices of Minority and Women Inclusion and Diversity Standards

All federal financial agencies and all Reserve Banks have established an OMWI. Six of the seven agencies that existed when the Dodd-Frank Act was enacted established OMWIs by January 2011, pursuant to the time frame established in the act. Additionally, SEC formally established its OMWI in July 2011, following House and Senate Appropriations Committees' approvals of the agency's request to create an OMWI.[32] SEC selected an OMWI director in December 2011, who officially joined the office in January 2012. CFPB, which assumed responsibility for certain consumer financial protection functions in July 2011, established its OMWI in January 2012 and its OMWI director officially joined the agency in April 2012.[33]

Many agencies and most of the Reserve Banks established their OMWIs as new, separate offices. Four of eight agencies and 9 of 12 Reserve Banks established their OMWIs separate from other offices, including four banks that refocused existing diversity offices as their OMWIs. Three agencies—FDIC, the Federal Reserve Board, and OCC—and three banks—the Reserve Banks of Atlanta, Kansas City, and Philadelphia— established their OMWIs within existing offices of equal employment opportunity (EEO) or diversity. FHFA established its OMWI and then merged its EEO function into that office. OMWI officials from several agencies with separate OMWIs said their staff worked with their EEO offices to address agency diversity issues. Similarly, many agency and Reserve Bank OMWI officials said they coordinated with other offices across their organizations, such as human resources, recruiting, procurement, and management, to support ongoing diversity and inclusion efforts organizationwide.

Federal financial agencies and Reserve Banks all have taken steps to staff their OMWIs. As of January 2013, the agencies had allocated between 3 and 40 full-time equivalent positions to their OMWIs (see table 3), and all agencies had open positions they planned to fill among these allocated positions. FDIC had allocated 40 full-time equivalent positions to its combined OMWI/EEO office as of January 2013. Many of FDIC's OMWI staff, including eight EEO specialists, support the office's EEO functions, and OCC and FHFA also reported EEO specialists among their staff. The agency OMWIs included directors and analysts among their staff, as well as some positions specific to certain functions of the OMWIs. For example, four of the agencies—CFPB, FDIC, NCUA, and SEC—had allocated staff specifically to recruitment and outreach functions, and four of the agencies—NCUA, OCC, SEC, and Treasury— had allocated staff specifically to business and supplier diversity. Four agencies—the Federal Reserve Board, FHFA, NCUA, and OCC—had each allocated a position to help implement the Dodd-Frank Act requirement to review the diversity practices of regulated entities. Additionally, two of the agencies—CFPB and SEC—had attorney positions among their OMWI staff.

Table 3. OMWI Staffing Levels for Federal Financial Agencies, as of January 2013

Agency	Allocated	Filled
CFPB	4	3
Federal Reserve Board[a]	3	2
FDIC[a]	40	35
FHFA a,b	9	8
NCUA	6	5
OCC[a]	12	11
SEC c	9	8
Treasury	11	8

Source: GAO analysis of federal financial agency information.

[a]Totals for FDIC, FHFA, and OCC include EEO staff, as the OMWI offices for these agencies include both functions. The Federal Reserve Board also established its OMWI within an existing office, but it provided information for OMWI staff only and excluded the office's director position, as agency officials said additional funds for the director position were not allocated because the director's primary duties included overseeing EEO compliance, diversity, and inclusion.

[b]Totals for FHFA include part-time staff.

[c]In addition to these staff, SEC's OMWI is supported by two full-time contract positions, a program analyst and a recruitment coordinator.

The Reserve Banks had allocated between three and seven full-time equivalent positions to their OMWIs as of January 2013 (see table 4). Ten of the 12 Reserve Banks had filled all of these positions, while the Reserve Banks of Cleveland and St. Louis each had one open position. The Reserve Bank OMWIs included directors and analysts among their staff. Few Reserve Banks designated specific OMWI functions to certain positions. Three banks, the Reserve Banks of Atlanta, Boston, and St. Louis, had each allocated one position to supplier or business diversity, and two other banks, the Reserve Banks of Chicago and Cleveland, had each allocated one position to help carry out the reporting functions of the OMWIs.

Perspectives on the role of OMWIs varied across some Reserve Bank officials with whom we spoke. While several Reserve Bank officials said their OMWIs were involved in policy development with a commitment to improving the Reserve Bank's diversity efforts over time, officials from one Reserve Bank said their OMWI was compliance-focused and primarily analyzed the banks' human capital resources and recruiting functions for compliance with Dodd-Frank Act requirements. Reserve Bank of Dallas officials told us they considered the OMWI staff members as objective critics of the Reserve Bank's recruitment, procurement, and financial education efforts, and that bank management is responsible for fostering diversity and inclusion across the organization.

Table 4. OMWI Staffing Levels for Reserve Banks, as of January 2013

Reserve Bank	Allocated	Filled
Atlanta[a]	4.5	4.5
Boston	5	5
Chicago	7	7
Cleveland	4	3
Dallas[b]	4	4
Kansas City[b]	5	5
Minneapolis[b]	3	3
New York	5	5
Philadelphia[b]	3	3
Richmond	5	5
San Francisco	3	3
St. Louis	5	4

Source: GAO analysis of Reserve Bank information.
[a]Totals for the Reserve Bank of Atlanta include part-time staff.
[b]Totals for the Reserve Banks of Dallas, Kansas City, Minneapolis, and Philadelphia include full-time employees with shared duties that help support the OMWI.

The act also required federal financial agency and Reserve Bank OMWIs to develop standards for equal employment opportunity and the racial, ethnic, and gender diversity of the workforce and senior management.[34] Six of eight agencies and most Reserve Banks indicated either their previously established equal employment opportunity standards or MD-715 requirements for agencies helped satisfy the Dodd-Frank Act requirement to establish equal employment opportunity standards with minimal changes, while two agencies and one Reserve Bank were still determining how to respond to the requirement. Treasury and CFPB planned to develop benchmarks of best practices as standards for diversity and inclusion. For example, Treasury officials said they planned to identify qualitative measures or indicators for assessing workforce diversity practices. Additionally, the Reserve Banks of Kansas City and San Francisco revised their diversity and inclusion policies pursuant to Dodd-Frank Act requirements. One agency established new standards separate from its existing equal employment opportunity policies as standards for the diversity of the workforce and senior management. Specifically, NCUA developed a diversity and inclusion strategic plan in response to a government-wide executive order that provides diversity standards and goals, which officials said the agency used to help establish expectations for staff.[35]

Agencies and Reserve Banks Are Implementing Recruitment Practices

OMWI Annual Reports to Congress and officials we contacted indicated that federal financial agencies and Reserve Banks have implemented various practices pursuant to the Dodd-Frank Act's requirements regarding diversity recruiting, outlined in table 5. Most agency and Reserve Bank OMWIs indicated that they had been conducting various diversity recruitment practices prior to the enactment of the Dodd-Frank Act—such as partnering with organizations focused on developing opportunities for minorities and women.

Table 5. Federal Financial Agency and Reserve Bank Implementation of Dodd-Frank Act Section 342 Diversity Recruitment Requirements

Section	Requirement	Agency and Reserve Bank implementation efforts
Sec. 342(f)(1)	Recruiting at historically black colleges and universities, Hispanic-serving institutions, women's colleges, and colleges that typically serve majority minority populations	Seven of eight agencies and all Reserve Banks reported on efforts to recruit from historically black colleges and universities and other minority-serving institutions. Additionally, a few Reserve Banks reported on regional diversity recruitment efforts that included recruiting from two California State University locations that serve Latino communities.
Sec. 342(f)(2)	Sponsoring and recruiting at job fairs in urban communities	All agencies and all Reserve Banks participated in diversity job fairs sponsored by minority-serving groups. These practices included participating in national job fairs sponsored by the National Urban League, National Black MBA Association, National Association of Black Accountants, National Society of Hispanic MBAs, Association of LatinoProfessionals in Finance and Accounting, Society for Women Engineers, National Association of Asian MBAs, and the Pacific Asian Consortium in Employment.

Section	Requirement	Agency and Reserve Bank implementation efforts
Sec. 342(f)(3)	Placing employment advertisements in newspapers and magazines oriented toward minorities and women	Five agencies and all Reserve Banks reported on efforts to place advertisements in minority- and women-serving publications. These included posting jobs in IMDiversity, Hispanic Business, EOE Journal, Diversity Life, Diversity Women, and Hispanic Life magazines.
Sec. 342(f)(4)	Partnering with organizations focused on developing opportunities for minorities and women to place talented young minorities and women in industry internships, summer employment, and full-time positions	Seven agencies and all Reserve Banks have partnerships with organizations for internship programs, including the Hispanic Association of Colleges and Universities, Washington Internships for Native Students, and INROADS, a nonprofit organization that trains and develops minority students for careers in business and industry.
Sec. 342(f)(6)	Any other mass media communications that the OMWI determines necessary	Two agencies and all Reserve Banks identified additional mass media communications to support their diversity recruiting efforts, including using social media networking sites such as Facebook and Twitter to reach diverse candidates. For example, CFPB created a recruitment website based on the agency's review of best practices for developing diverse applicant pools, and the Federal Reserve System (the Board and all the Reserve Banks) maintains a presence on the LinkedIn networking website.

Source: GAO summary of Dodd-Frank Act section 342 and information provided by federal financial agencies and Reserve Banks.

Note: Sec. 342(f)(5) pertains to partnering with inner-city high schools, girls' high schools, and majority-minority population high schools to establish or enhance financial literacy programs and provide mentoring and is not included in this list or addressed in this report.

The majority of agencies and Reserve Banks focused their recruitment efforts on attending job fairs and maintaining partnerships with minority-serving institutions and organizations. According to Federal Reserve Board and Reserve Bank officials, they collectively participate in and fund recruitment activities, including national career fairs, advertisements in diverse publications, and social media initiatives. The Reserve Bank of Chicago coordinates the Federal Reserve System's participation in national diversity recruitment events and oversees an internal training initiative aimed at developing and retaining employees within the Federal Reserve System. In addition to participating in these efforts, Reserve Banks conduct some activities independently.

Some OMWIs indicated their diversity activities had changed due in part to recent efforts to satisfy section 342 requirements as well as broadening their approaches to diversity and inclusion. For example, some OMWIs indicated the scope of their diversity and inclusion practices had broadened to include persons with disabilities as well as the lesbian, gay, bisexual, and transgender community. Further, the majority of OMWIs reported on plans to improve or expand existing practices. For example, many OMWIs described plans to pursue new or further develop existing partnerships with organizations focused on developing opportunities for minorities and women, and some OMWIs described recent efforts to expand internship opportunities for minority students.

Some OMWI officials identified practices targeted to improve organizationwide diversity, which could eventually help build management-level diversity. These included targeted recruitment to attract minorities and women, training for hiring managers and other employees on diversity hiring practices, and expanded internship programs as a way to hire a greater number of female and minority interns.

- *Targeted recruitment.* All agencies and Reserve Banks with whom we spoke had participated in career fairs or partnerships with minority-serving organizations, as outlined in section 342 of the Dodd-Frank Act, to target diversity recruitment, and in several cases bolster recruitment of particular populations, such as Hispanics. The OMWIs at FDIC, FHFA, and SEC work with the agencies' hiring and recruitment staff to identify strategies for recruiting diverse candidates. Additionally, the Federal Reserve Board OMWI reported that including hiring managers at diversity career fairs had made their targeted recruitment activities more effective.

- *Training for hiring managers.* Some OMWIs reported they implemented practices to educate supervisors and hiring managers on diversity hiring practices. For example, the Reserve Bank of New York designed a training course to enhance cross-cultural interviewing skills of recruitment staff. OCC also provides diversity recruitment training to the agency's recruitment staff, and CFPB planned to provide its hiring managers a toolkit with tips on diversity hiring practices.

- *Internship programs.* Many agencies and Reserve Banks implemented internship programs to build employment diversity by developing a more diverse pipeline of potential entry-level candidates. For example, the Reserve Bank of San Francisco reported that it expanded its internship program to support more interns and leveraged partnerships with organizations representing minorities and women to increase the diversity of the bank's internship program applicant pool.

Agencies Have Taken Preliminary Steps to Develop Procedures to Assess Diversity Policies and Practices of Regulated Entities

In response to section 342 of the Dodd-Frank Act, seven federal financial agencies have taken preliminary steps to respond to the requirement to develop standards for assessing the diversity policies and practices of entities they oversee. While these agencies have made initial progress, it is too soon to evaluate how effectively the agencies are responding to this requirement. The affected agencies include CFPB, FDIC, FHFA, the Federal Reserve Board, NCUA, OCC, and SEC.[36] In addition to this requirement under the Dodd-Frank Act, FHFA is also subject to the Housing and Economic Recovery Act of 2008 (HERA), under which it must assess its regulated entities' diversity activities and meet other provisions similar to those in section 342.[37]

In 2010, FHFA developed an agency regulation implementing HERA requirements, in part, to ensure that diversity is a component of all aspects of its regulated entities' business activities. The agency's regulated entities include Fannie Mae, Freddie Mac, Federal Home Loan Banks, and the Federal Home Loan Bank System's Office of Finance. HERA requires the agency's regulated entities to develop diversity policies and procedures, staff an OMWI, and report annually to FHFA on their OMWI activities, among other requirements.[38] In addition, FHFA has enforcement authority under HERA and FHFA's promulgated regulation to ensure its regulated entities have diversity standards in place. According to FHFA OMWI officials, the agency's response to HERA also satisfies the section 342 requirement.

According to OMWI officials, other agencies reviewed FHFA's regulation as a possible option for responding to the section 342 requirement; however, the enforcement authority included in FHFA's regulation is unique to the agency. They said that under the Dodd-Frank Act their agencies do not have enforcement authority to require regulated entities to implement diversity standards and practices. [39] Officials from the affected agencies also told us their OMWIs collaborated on initial steps to determine how to respond to these requirements by meeting periodically as a group, meeting with members of Congress, and performing outreach to industry participants and advocacy groups.

The agency OMWI directors began meeting periodically in 2011 and began in 2012 to explore the possibility of developing a uniform set of standards that agencies could use as a baseline for developing standards for assessing the diversity practices of their regulated entities. Agency OMWI officials said the working group aimed to develop a set of standards for review and feedback from industry participants. As part of these efforts, some OMWI directors of the affected agencies participated in meetings with members of Congress to explore issues involving collection and analysis of workforce diversity data. Some members of the working group also held meetings with industry and advocacy groups to understand industry views on developing standards for assessing diversity policies and practices. One OMWI reported that industry representatives discussed options for evaluating diversity with respect to a regulated entity's size, complexity, and market area.

OMWI officials told us responding to the requirement was a challenge for several reasons. Specifically, differences across regulated entities in terms of size, complexity, and market area made it challenging to develop a uniform standard. Determining the process and format for developing standards was also a challenge. OMWI officials also said they want to minimize adding a new regulatory burden to meet this provision. Therefore, the agencies would like to leverage existing information sources—data that regulated entities already provide—in evaluating the diversity activities of regulated entities. For example, to find ways to avoid duplicating existing data-collection efforts, CFPB and NCUA were working with EEOC for access to EEO-1 data for regulated entities. OCC officials said OCC had also considered using EEO-1 data, but some regulated entities had concerns about maintaining proprietary information, given the potential for Freedom of Information Act requests.[40]

Efforts to Report on Measuring Outcomes and Progress Could Be Enhanced

In addition to establishing an OMWI, the act required federal financial agencies and Reserve Banks to report annually on their diversity practices, and nearly all of the agencies and all the Reserve Banks have begun reporting annually on their diversity practices. As discussed earlier, the act required each

OMWI to submit to Congress an annual report on the actions taken pursuant to section 342, including information on the percentage of amounts paid to minority-and women-owned contractors and successes and challenges in recruiting and hiring qualified minority and women employees, and other information as the OMWI director determines appropriate. Including more information on the outcomes and progress of their diversity practices could enhance the usefulness of these annual reports. Seven of eight agencies and all Reserve Banks issued annual reports in 2011. CFPB, which was created in July 2010 and assumed responsibility for certain consumer financial protection functions in July 2011, issued an agencywide semiannual report for 2011. Its OMWI planned to issue an annual report for 2012 at the same time as the other agencies, in March 2013.

In their 2011 Annual OMWI Reports to Congress, several agencies and Reserve Banks reported on efforts to measure outcomes and progress of various diversity practices, which provide examples of the types of outcomes and measures of progress that could be helpful for OMWIs to include in their annual reports. Although the act requires information on successes and challenges, it does not specifically require reporting on effectiveness; however, the act provides some leeway to the federal financial agencies and the Reserve Banks to include "any other information, findings, conclusions, and recommendations for legislative or agency action, as the Director determines appropriate."[41] Measurement of diversity practices is one of the nine leading diversity management practices we previously identified. We have reported that quantitative measures—such as tracking employment demographic statistics—and qualitative measures—such as evaluating employee feedback survey results—could help organizations translate their diversity aspirations into tangible practice.[42]

The Federal Reserve Board reported that it tracks job applicant information to assess the diversity of applicant pools, candidates interviewed, and employees hired as a result of diversity recruiting efforts, and FDIC reported that it monitors participation and attrition rates and diversity characteristics of participants in a development program. SEC reported plans to develop standards for assessing its ongoing diversity and inclusion efforts and include them in a strategic plan. The Reserve Banks of Chicago, Philadelphia, Richmond, and San Francisco reported on the number of internships each bank supported and the ethnic and gender diversity of the interns. The Reserve Bank of Chicago also reported on the number of job offers extended and candidates hired from its internship program, as well as on the number of candidates successfully hired from a diversity career expo.

Further, the Reserve Bank of Cleveland identified reporting tools developed to monitor the bank's inclusion in contracting efforts. In addition to using these measures, some OMWI officials said they used annual employee surveys as a measurement tool to gather information about the progress of their diversity practices, including retention practices. For example, FDIC's annual employee survey includes specific questions related to diversity, and the agency uses responses to assess the effectiveness of policies and programs and outline action steps for improvement. OCC officials told us the government-wide federal employee viewpoint survey provided information on employee perspectives about diversity, and the agency measured its results against government-wide scores. Further, OMWI officials from the Reserve Bank of Minneapolis said exit surveys and employee declination surveys provided additional information for evaluating their retention and recruiting programs.

Federal financial agencies and Reserve Banks have focused their initial OMWI efforts on implementing section 342 of the Dodd-Frank Act. While many OMWIs have implemented or are planning efforts to measure and evaluate the progress of their diversity and inclusion activities, which is consistent with the leading diversity management practices, information on such efforts is not yet reported consistently across the OMWI annual reports. According to OMWI officials as well as industry representatives we interviewed, measuring the progress of diversity recruitment and retention practices is a challenging, long-term process. For example, NCUA officials told us measuring the progress of certain recruiting practices could be a challenge, as access to demographic information about job applicants might be limited. Additionally, FHFA officials told us that while measuring the progress of diversity practices was needed to identify best practices, such measurement needs to be efficient and meaningful. However, without knowledge of OMWI efforts to measure outcomes and the progress of their diversity practices, Congress lacks information that would help hold OMWIs accountable for achieving desired outcomes. In addition, increased attention to evaluation and measurement through annual reporting of these efforts could help the OMWIs improve management of their diversity practices. Reporting such information would provide an opportunity for the agencies and Reserve Banks to learn from others' efforts to measure their progress and indicate areas for improvement.

PROCEDURES TO MEET DODD-FRANK INCLUSIVE CONTRACTING REQUIREMENTS ARE LARGELY IN PLACE

Section 342 of the Dodd-Frank Act requires federal financial agencies and Reserve Banks to develop procedures to ensure, to the maximum extent possible, the fair inclusion and utilization of women and minorities in contracting. Specifically, the act requires agency and Reserve Bank actions to ensure that its contractors are making efforts to include women and minorities in their workforce. Also, the act has requirements for actions to increase contracting opportunities for minority- and women-owned businesses (MWOB).[43] Most agencies and Reserve Banks have developed and included a provision in contracts for services requiring their contractors to make efforts to ensure the fair inclusion of women and minorities in their workforce and subcontracted workforces. The extent to which these agencies and Reserve Banks have contracted with MWOBs varied widely. These entities reported multiple challenges to increasing contracting opportunities for MWOBs and used various technical assistance practices to address these challenges.

Most Agencies and Reserve Banks Are Implementing Requirements Related to Inclusiveness in Contractor Workforces

To address the act's requirement to ensure the fair inclusion of women and minorities, to the maximum extent possible, in contracted workforces, agencies either have developed or are in the process of developing fair inclusion provisions in their contracts for services, and all Reserve Banks have done so. In addition, some agencies and all Reserve Banks have developed procedures to assess contractors' efforts for workforce inclusion of women and minorities.

Fair Inclusion Provision in Contracts

Five agencies—FDIC, FHFA, NCUA, OCC, and the Federal Reserve Board—and all Reserve Banks have created a fair inclusion provision and are using it in contracts for services. Section 342 of the Dodd-Frank Act requires agencies and Reserve Banks to develop procedures for review and evaluation of contract proposals for services and for hiring service providers that include a written statement that the contractor, and as applicable subcontractors, shall ensure, to the maximum extent possible, the fair inclusion of women and minorities in the workforce of the contractor and, as applicable, subcontractors. The act does not specify the elements to be included in the written statement and provides that each OMWI director prescribe the form and content of the statement.

CFPB, SEC, and Treasury are each in the process of developing a fair inclusion provision. CFPB is developing procurement procedures to address the requirements of the act and required more time because its OMWI office was established in January 2012. SEC is subject to the Federal Acquisition Regulation (FAR) and is currently developing its inclusive contract provision.[44] While CFPB and SEC develop inclusion statements pursuant to the act, both agencies have been using the equal employment opportunity statement contained in the FAR in executed contracts. Treasury has developed its fair inclusion provision to add to future contracts. It has issued a notice of proposed rulemaking in the Federal Register for public comments on this change to its contracting procedures as required under the law. The comment period ended on October 22, 2012. Treasury received eight comments which included, among other things, suggestions to make the fair inclusion provision applicable to all contracts regardless of the dollar amount of the contract and to better specify the documentation required of contractors to demonstrate that they have met the requirements of the fair inclusion provision. Treasury is currently reviewing the public comments and considering changes to the proposed rule.

The fair inclusion provisions we reviewed contained the following:

- *Equal employment opportunity statement:* Fair inclusion provisions include a commitment by the contractor to equal opportunity in employment and contracting and, to the maximum extent possible consistent with applicable law, the fair inclusion of women and minorities in the contractor's workforce.
- *Documentation:* To enforce the fair inclusion provision, agencies require contractors to provide documentation of their efforts to include women and minorities in the contractor's workforce, such as a written affirmative action plan; documentation of the number of employees by race, ethnicity, and gender; information on subcontract awards, including whether the subcontractor is an MWOB; and any other actions describing the contractor's efforts toward the inclusion of women and minorities.

- *Contract amount threshold:* Agencies apply the fair inclusion provision to contracts exceeding a certain dollar amount. For two agencies subject to the act, this threshold is any amount over $150,000. For three agencies subject to the act, this threshold is any amount over $100,000. The Reserve Bank fair inclusion provisions we reviewed did not generally include a dollar-amount threshold.

None of the officials from five agencies that have implemented a fair inclusion provision required by the act described to us receiving an adverse reaction from contractors, but officials from a majority of the Reserve Banks we spoke with described resistance or concerns from some contractors. OCC stated that smaller businesses had expressed confusion about the requirement because the businesses are too small to report workforce demographics to EEOC. Eight Reserve Banks described contractors expressing some disagreement or concern at the inclusion of the language in contracts. According to some Reserve Bank officials, contractors were concerned that accepting the fair inclusion provision would trigger other federal requirements for their businesses, or subject the contractor to meeting hiring or subcontracting targets.[45] Some Reserve Banks described explaining the limited scope of the provision to concerned contractors. Other Reserve Banks described modifying the language in the fair inclusion provision, for example, in one case, changing a phrase regarding the contractor's efforts to include women and minorities from "to the maximum extent possible" to read "to the maximum extent required by law." Other Reserve Banks described occurrences where, in response to a contractor's concern, they excluded the fair inclusion language from contracts for a procurement with a small dollar amount or because the vendor provided a service critical to the Reserve Bank and alternate vendors were not available.[46] Finally, one Reserve Bank described declining a contract and seeking an alternate vendor that accepted the provision.

Procedures to Assess Contractors' Inclusion Efforts

Some agencies and all Reserve Banks have developed procedures to assess contractors' efforts toward workforce inclusion of women and minorities. Section 342 of the Dodd-Frank Act requires the 8 federal financial agencies in the act and 12 Reserve Banks to develop procedures to determine whether a contractor and, as applicable, a subcontractor, has failed to make a good faith effort to include minorities and women in their workforces. Good faith efforts include any actions intended to identify and remove barriers to employment or to expand employment opportunities for minorities and women in the workplace, according to the policies some agencies have developed. For example, recruiting minorities and women or providing these groups job training may be considered good faith efforts for diversity inclusion. Contractors must certify that they have made a good faith effort to include women and minorities in their workforces, according to most policies we reviewed. At the same time, contractors may provide documentation of their inclusion efforts such as workforce demographics, subcontract recipients, and the contractor's plan to ensure that women and minorities have opportunities to enter and advance within its workforce. Agencies and Reserve Banks plan to conduct a review of each contractor's certifications and documentation annually, once in a 2-year period, or at other times deemed necessary, such as when contracts are executed or renewed, to make a determination of whether the contractor made a good faith effort to include women and minorities in its workforce. Failure to make a good faith effort may result in termination of the contract, referral to the Office of Federal Contract Compliance Programs, or other appropriate action.[47] Four agencies and all Reserve Banks have established good faith effort determination procedures, and four agencies have yet to implement such procedures.

Levels of Contracting with Minority- and Women-Owned Businesses Varied by Agency and Reserve Bank

In 2011, the proportion of a federal financial agency's contracting dollars awarded to businesses owned by minorities or women varied, ranging between 12 percent and 38 percent according to the OMWI reports of the agencies (see fig. 14).[48] Seven federal financial agencies awarded a total of about $2.4 billion for contracting for external goods and services in fiscal year 2011, with FDIC awarding about $1.4 billion of this amount.

Similarly, according to Reserve Bank OMWI reports, Reserve Bank contracting dollars paid to businesses owned by minorities or women ranged between 3 percent and 24 percent in 2011 (see fig. 15). Reserve Banks paid about $897 million in fiscal year 2011 in contracting.

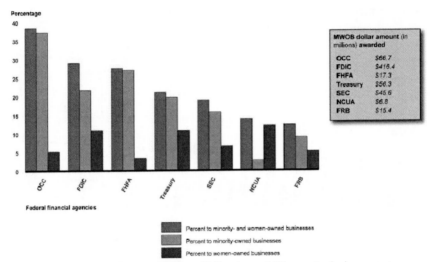

Source: GAO review of agency Office of Minority and Women Inclusion reports.

Note: CFPB was not required to issue an OMWI report to Congress in 2011. Percentages of dollar amounts awarded to minority-owned businesses and women-owned businesses displayed separately may not be mutually exclusive for all agencies and do not always total to the combined percent to minority- and women-owned business category. Some businesses are both minority- and women-owned and may be counted by agencies under both categories.

Figure 14. Dollar Amount and Percentage of Total Awarded to Minority- and Women-Owned Businesses (MWOB) by Agency, 2011.

Among federal financial agencies, OCC awarded the largest proportional amount of contracting dollars to MWOBs—about 38 percent (almost $67 million). OCC officials told us that its contract needs tend to be for services for which there is often a pool of MWOB suppliers and most of OCC's 2011 contract dollars were spent on computer related services. The Federal Reserve Board awarded the smallest proportion of its contracting dollars to MWOBs, with about 12 percent going to such businesses. According to the Federal Reserve Board, a significant amount of its procurement is for economic data, which are generally not available from MWOBs. Although federal agencies are not generally required to report on MWOBs, most are required to report on certain small business contracting goals, including goals for women and small disadvantaged businesses (which include minority-owned businesses).[49] In a 2012 report, we found that 35 percent of funds all federal agencies obligated to small businesses in 2011 were obligated to minority-owned small businesses and 17 percent were obligated to women-owned businesses.[50]

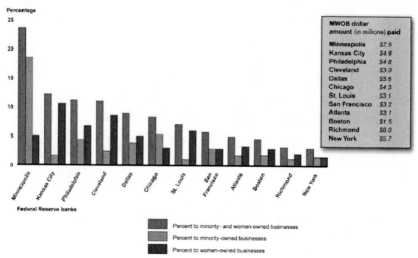

Source: GAO review of Federal Reserve Bank Office of Minority and Women Inclusion reports.

Note: Reserve Banks reported amounts paid to contractors in OMWI reports rather than amounts awarded as reported by agencies.

Figure 15. Dollar Amount and Percentage of Total Paid to Minority- and Women-Owned Businesses (MWOB) by Reserve Bank, 2011.

Among Reserve Banks, the Reserve Bank of Minneapolis paid the largest proportion of its contracting dollars to MWOBs with about 24 percent going to such businesses (18.5 percent to minority-owned businesses and about 5 percent to women-owned businesses). According to the Reserve Bank of Minneapolis, almost half of its MWOB contract dollars were paid for software and related technology integration services from minority-owned firms. All other Reserve Banks paid under 13 percent of contracting dollars to MWOBs, with the Reserve Bank of New York awarding the smallest percentage of its contracting dollars to such businesses (3 percent). The Reserve Bank of New York described its commitment to increasing diversity in its pool of potential contractors through its outreach efforts to us and in its 2011 OMWI report. For example, the Reserve Bank of New York held an event with its primary contractors and small firms to identify potential partnerships and an event that provided small firms consultation on business plans and credit applications to increase the capacity of the small firms.

Agencies and Reserve Banks Report Challenges to Increasing Contracting Opportunities and Have Offered Technical Assistance to Minority- and Women-Owned Businesses

Seven federal financial agencies included in this report and all 12 Reserve Banks identified challenges in increasing contracting opportunities for MWOBs. Section 342 of the Dodd-Frank Act requires federal financial agencies and Reserve Banks to include in their annual OMWI report a description of the challenges they may face in contracting with qualified MWOBs. As a new agency, CFPB has not been required to complete an annual OMWI report and did not identify any contracting challenges to us. In interviews with us and in the 2011 OMWI reports to Congress, the remaining agencies and all Reserve Banks discussed a number of common challenges to increasing contracting with MWOBs, including the following:

- *Limited capacity of MWOBs:* Some agencies and Reserve Banks stated that reporting or other requirements under federal contracts were often too great a burden for MWOBs or that MWOBs needed to build capacity to meet federal contracting requirements. Some agencies and Reserve Banks also stated that at times the need for goods or services is not scaled to the capacity of MWOBs. For example, some agencies and Reserve Banks faced challenges identifying MWOBs that can meet procurement needs on a national scale.
- *Developing staff or procedures to meet contracting requirements of the act:* According to some agencies, new OMWIs require additional staff or staff development, or procedures to meet the requirements of the act, including providing technical assistance to increase opportunities for MWOBs, identifying qualified MWOBs in the marketplace, and incorporating the use of a fair inclusion provision in contracts and good faith effort determination processes, which we discussed earlier, into established procurement processes.
- *MWOB classification challenges:* Multiple agencies and Reserve Banks described difficulty identifying and classifying suppliers as diverse entities. Some Reserve Banks noted that no central agency is

responsible for certifying MWOBs. Some agencies and Reserve Banks also discussed a need for new procedures or information systems to identify and classify diverse ownership of businesses.

- *Availability:* Some agencies and Reserve Banks noted that specialized services are often only available from a limited pool of suppliers that may not include MWOBs.

- *Centralized procurement:* Reserve Banks may use the National Procurement Office (NPO), the centralized procurement office for the 12 Reserve Banks, to contract for some goods and services.[51] When a Reserve Bank procures through the NPO, access to MWOBs may be limited because the NPO procures for volume discounts with larger contractors. However, the Reserve Bank of Richmond, in its 2011 OMWI report, described efforts to work with existing large contractors to increase subcontracting with smaller, diverse firms.

- *No MWOB bids:* In some cases, agencies and Reserve Banks found that potentially eligible MWOB applicants decided not to bid without explanation.

Other challenges were described on a limited basis by one agency or Reserve Bank. For example, NCUA explained that MWOBs are not familiar with the agency. According to NCUA, to address this issue it increased its outreach budget and attendance to MWOB events and published an online guide on doing business with the agency. According to FDIC, in some cases MWOBs do not have relationships with large federal contractors for subcontracting opportunities. To address this problem, FDIC emphasizes to larger firms the importance of subcontracting with MWOBs and has negotiated increases in MWOB subcontracting participation with large contractors. FDIC participated in procurement events where small and large contractors could meet and match capabilities. The Reserve Bank of Chicago stated that MWOBs have a hard time standing out in highly competitive industries, such as staff augmentation services. Finally, according to the Reserve Bank of Richmond, MWOBs may have incorrect perceptions that Reserve Banks are subject to federal procurement rules that they cannot meet.

To counter challenges MWOBs may face in accessing federal contracting opportunities, all agencies and Reserve Banks described providing various specific forms of technical assistance to MWOBs, which they described in discussions with us and in 2011 OMWI reports to Congress.

No agency or Reserve Bank stood out as coordinating technical assistance better than others, although some agencies pointed to longstanding efforts at

FDIC to provide technical assistance to MWOBs as model practices. Section 342 of the Dodd-Frank Act requires federal financial agencies and Reserve Banks to develop standards for coordinating technical assistance to MWOBs. These activities included developing and distributing literature, such as manuals and brochures describing contracting procedures and resources to prospective contractors. Most agencies also established websites that function as informational portals on doing business with agencies and act as an agency entry point to prospective contractors. Agencies and Reserve Banks described outreach activities to MWOBs, including conducting expert panels, hosting meetings and workshops, and exhibiting at trade shows and procurement events. Some of these outreach activities have been coordinated with SBA. For example, FDIC has partnered with SBA to develop a technical assistance program for small businesses, including MWOBs, on money management. OCC worked with SBA to create a technical assistance workshop that they conducted in 2012 with women-owned small businesses. Some agencies have included SBA representatives in supplier diversity events they sponsor. Even prior to the passage of the Dodd-Frank Act, the Federal Reserve Board had participated in SBA procurement fairs and used SBA information and events to market its procurement opportunities among diverse suppliers. Treasury has participated in SBA outreach events and created a mentor-protégé program to assist small businesses with contracting opportunities.[52]

Agencies and Reserve Banks also provide one-on-one technical assistance, which is intended to meet the specific needs of a prospective MWOB contractor. According to Treasury, they coordinate with SBA to leverage SBA's knowledge of one-on-one technical assistance practices with MWOBs. FHFA and SEC have created dedicated e-mail addresses and telephone lines for MWOBs to reach their OMWIs, and SEC has established monthly vendor outreach days when MWOBs can speak one-on-one with SEC's supplier diversity officer and small-business specialist. Some Reserve Banks described conducting one-on-one meetings with prospective contractors in 2011, some of which were held during procurement events. Finally, FDIC offered its database of MWOBs to the OMWIs and some agencies described using or planning to use it to identify potential contractors for outreach regarding procurement opportunities. According to FDIC, it sends an updated version of the database to the agencies each quarter.

CONCLUSION

Across financial services firms, federal financial agencies, and Reserve Banks, available data showed the representation of minorities and women varied, and there was little overall change in workforce diversity from 2007 through 2011. Our findings suggest the overall diversity of the financial services industry has generally remained steady following the financial crisis. Since 2011, federal financial agencies and Reserve Banks have taken initial steps to respond to the Dodd-Frank Act's requirements to promote workforce diversity, and OMWIs have begun reporting on both planned and existing diversity practices, in addition to reporting on workforce demographic statistics according to EEOC requirements. While many OMWIs have implemented or are planning efforts to measure and evaluate the progress of their diversity and inclusion activities, a leading diversity management practice, information on these efforts is not reported consistently across the OMWI annual reports. Although the act requires information on successes and challenges, it does not specifically require reporting on measurement; however, the act provides that the federal financial agencies and the Reserve Banks can include additional information determined appropriate by the OMWI director. Measurement of diversity practices is one of the nine leading diversity management practices we have previously identified. Reporting on these efforts as part of annual OMWI reporting would provide Congress, other OMWIs, and the financial services industry with potentially useful information on the ongoing implementation of diversity practices. Such information could be helpful industrywide, as management-level diversity at federal financial agencies, Reserve Banks, and the broader financial services industry continues to be largely unchanged. Without information on OMWI efforts to report outcomes and the progress of diversity and inclusion practices, Congress lacks information that would help hold agencies accountable for achieving desired outcomes or whether OMWI efforts are having any impact.

RECOMMENDATIONS FOR EXECUTIVE ACTION

To enhance the availability of information on the progress and impact of agency and Reserve Bank diversity practices, we are recommending to CFPB, FDIC, the Federal Reserve Board, FHFA, NCUA, OCC, SEC, Treasury, and the Reserve Banks that each OMWI report on efforts to measure the progress of its employment diversity and inclusion practices, including measurement outcomes as appropriate, to indicate areas for improvement as part of their annual reports to Congress.

AGENCY COMMENTS AND OUR EVALUATION

We provided drafts of this report to CFPB, the Federal Reserve Board, FDIC, FHFA, NCUA, OCC, SEC, Treasury, and each of the Federal Reserve Banks for review and comment. We received written comments from each of the agencies and a consolidated letter from all of the Reserve Banks. The agencies and Reserve Banks generally agreed with our recommendation. CFPB, Federal Reserve Banks, FDIC, FHFA, NCUA, OCC, and SEC provided technical comments, which we incorporated as appropriate. We also provided a draft of the report to EEOC for comment. EEOC is not subject to the requirements of section 342 of the act but did provide technical comments, which we incorporated as appropriate.

With respect to our recommendation that each OMWI report on efforts to measure the progress of its employment diversity and inclusion practices, including measurement outcomes as appropriate, to indicate areas for improvement as part of their annual reports to Congress, all the federal financial agencies and Reserve Banks indicated that they plan to implement the recommendation:

- the OMWI Director of CFPB explained that its OMWI was the newest of such offices because the agency was created with the enactment of the Dodd-Frank Act and that it planned to include measurement information in future reports;
- the OMWI Director of the Federal Reserve Board stated that the recommendation was consistent with its ongoing practices and that it would look for additional ways to report on diversity practices;
- FDIC's OMWI Director agreed with the recommendation and stated that it will include efforts to measure the progress of its diversity practices in its annual reports to Congress;
- the Acting Associate Director of FHFA's OMWI stated that it would include measurement information in its 2013 OMWI report to Congress;

- the Executive Director of NCUA said the agency will work toward reporting on its efforts to measure the progress of workforce diversity and practices;
- the Comptroller of the Currency stated that OCC had a well-developed diversity and inclusion program through which the agency measures its progress and that OCC has included additional metrics in its 2013 OMWI report to Congress;
- SEC's OMWI Director noted that the agency plans to incorporate measurement information on its diversity and inclusion practices in its future OMWI reports to Congress;
- Treasury's OMWI Director agreed with our recommendation and stated that it was consistent with the agency's efforts to use more than demographic representation to measure the progress of diversity and inclusion efforts; and
- the Federal Reserve Banks' OMWI directors noted that the banks currently include some measurement information in annual reports and said that they will consider additional ways to measure and report on Reserve Banks' diversity practices.

Sincerely yours,
Daniel Garcia-Diaz
Director, Financial Markets and Community Investment

APPENDIX I: OBJECTIVES, SCOPE, AND METHODOLOGY

The objectives for this report were to examine (1) what available data show about how the diversity of the financial services industry workforce and how diversity practices taken by the industry have changed from 2007 through 2011; (2) what available data show about how diversity in the workforces of the federal financial agencies and the Federal Reserve Banks (Reserve Banks) has changed from 2007 through 2011; (3) how these federal financial agencies and Reserve Banks are implementing workforce diversity practices under section 342 of the Dodd-Frank Act, including the extent to which their workforce diversity practices have changed since the financial crisis; and (4) the status of federal financial agencies' and Reserve Banks' implementation of the contracting provisions of the Dodd-Frank Act related to the inclusion of women and minorities.

To describe how diversity in the financial services industry has changed since the beginning of the 2007-2009 financial crisis, we analyzed 2007- 2011 workforce data from the Equal Employment Opportunity Commission's (EEOC) Employer Information Report (EEO-1). EEO-1 is data annually submitted to EEOC generally by private-sector firms with more than 100 employees.[1] We obtained EEO-1 data on October 2012, from the finance and insurance industry categorized under the North American Industry Classification System (NAICS) code 52 for these industries from 2007 through 2011. EEO-1 data were specifically obtained from the EEOC's "officials and managers" category by gender, race/ethnicity, firm size, and industry sectors.[2] The EEO-1 "officials and managers" category was further divided into two management-level categories of first- and mid-level managers and senior-level managers and then analyzed by gender, race/ethnicity, and firm size.[3] To understand the potential internal candidate pools available for management positions in the financial industry, we obtained EEO-1 data under NAICS code 52 for all positions, including nonmanagement positions, by gender and race/ethnicity. To determine the reliability of the EEO-1 data that we received from EEOC, we interviewed knowledgeable EEOC officials and reviewed relevant documents provided by agency officials and obtained on its website. We also conducted electronic testing of the data. We determined that the EEO-1 data were sufficiently reliable for our purposes.

To corroborate the results of the EEO-1 data, we used an additional source of workforce diversity data from the Current Population Survey (CPS), a monthly survey of households the Bureau of the Census administers on behalf of the Bureau of Labor Statistics. CPS data provide information on labor force characteristics and demographic data, among other topics. Similar to the EEO-1 "officials and managers" job category, we used the CPS "management occupations" category—unlike EEO-1, CPS does not split its management into two levels—for our discussion of management-level diversity within the financial services industry. However, the statistics from these two sources are not exactly comparable. We determined the CPS-estimated percentages of minorities in management positions within the financial services industry could not be precisely measured. [4] See table 6 for the estimated percentages and standard errors. The standard errors for the minority percentages were greater than the standard errors for the white percentages, and they were relatively large compared to the estimated percentage for minorities. However, CPS minority percentages were included in this report for additional context. To determine the reliability of CPS data, which we obtained from a publicly accessible federal statistical database, we gathered and reviewed relevant documentation from the Bureau of the Census website, conducted electronic testing, and determined the standard errors of the CPS estimates. We determined that the CPS data were sufficiently reliable for our purposes.

Table 6. Estimated Percentages and Standard Errors for Race/Ethnicity in Management Positions in the Financial Services Industry Using the Current Population Survey (CPS), 2007-2011

Year	Race/ethnicity	Percentage	Standard errors
2007	White	85.9%	1.7%
2007	Minority	14.1	4.5
2008	White	85.9	1.7
2008	Minority	14.1	4.5
2009	White	83.1	1.9
2009	Minority	16.9	4.5
2010	White	86.0	1.8
2010	Minority	14.0	4.7
2011	White	84.9	1.8
2011	Minority	15.1	4.6

Source: GAO analysis of CPS data.

To gather information on a potential external pipeline of diverse candidates for management positions in the financial industry, we obtained demographic data on minority and female students enrolled in undergraduate, Master of Business Administration (MBA), and doctoral degree programs from 2007 through 2011 from the Association to Advance Collegiate Schools of Business (AACSB). We focused on MBA programs as a source of potential future managers and senior executives. Financial services firms compete for minorities in this pool with one another and with firms from other industries. We combined this information with undergraduate and doctoral degree programs to provide information on the overall diversity of the university system. AACSB conducts an annual voluntary survey called "Business School Questionnaire" of all its member schools. In 2011, AACSB updated its survey to include two additional race/ethnicity categories to include "two or more races" and "Native Hawaiian or Other Pacific Islander." For consistency purposes, we combined these two additional categories along with the representation of Native Americans into an "other" category. To determine the reliability of the AACSB data, we interviewed a knowledgeable AACSB official and reviewed relevant documents provided by the official and obtained on its website. We determined that the data from AACSB were sufficiently reliable for our purposes.

To determine how diversity practices in the financial services industry have changed since the beginning of the financial crisis, we conducted a literature review of relevant studies that discussed diversity best practices within the financial services industry from 2007 through 2011. In addition, we interviewed 10 selected industry representatives to determine whether the nine leading diversity practices we previously identified are relevant today and how diversity practices changed since 2007. We also reviewed documents produced by these industry representatives. These representatives were selected based on their participation in our previous work, suggestions from federal agencies we interviewed for this report, as well as the type of industry representative—such as an industry association or private firm.[5]

To describe diversity in the workforces of the federal financial agencies and Reserve Banks, we analyzed data we received from agencies and banks. To review changes in the representation of minorities and women in the workforces of federal financial agencies, we obtained from the agencies annual Equal Employment Opportunity Program Status Reports from 2007 through 2011, required under U.S. EEOC Management Directive 715 and known as MD-715 reports.[6] We obtained data from seven of the eight federal agencies required to meet the workforce diversity provisions in section 342 of the Dodd-Frank Wall Street Reform and Consumer Protection Act (Dodd-Frank Act). These included the Departmental Offices of the Department of the Treasury, the Federal Deposit Insurance Corporation, the Federal Housing Finance Agency (FHFA), the Board of Governors of the Federal Reserve System, the National Credit Union Administration, the Office of the Comptroller of the Currency, and the Securities and Exchange Commission. The Bureau of Consumer Financial Protection, commonly known as the Consumer Financial Protection Bureau (CFPB), was created in July 2010 and assumed responsibility for certain consumer financial protection functions in 2011; workforce diversity data for the agency to show trends from 2007 through 2011 were unavailable.[7] Additionally, our trend analysis excluded FHFA, as the agency was created in 2008 and did not report on diversity employment statistics for 2007, 2008, or 2009. Further, our senior management-level trend analysis excluded SEC, as the agency revised how it reported officials and managers during the 5-year period. To review changes in the representation of minorities and women in the workforces of Reserve Banks, we obtained from banks their annual EEO-1 reports from 2007 through 2011.[8] For agencies and Reserve Banks, we reviewed workplace employment data by occupational categories, distributed by race/ethnicity and gender.[9] In our analyses, we considered all categories other than white as race/ethnic minorities and analyzed trends in diversity at both the senior management-level and agency- and bankwide.[10] We analyzed senior management-level and overall diversity trends across all agencies and all Reserve Banks, as well as diversity trends for each agency when trend information was available.

To assess the reliability of MD-715 and EEO-1 data we received from agencies and Reserve Banks, we interviewed EEOC officials on both types of data as well as agency officials on MD-715 data and Reserve Bank officials on EEO-1 data about how the data are collected and verified as well as to identify potential data limitations. We found that while agencies and banks rely on employees to provide their race and ethnicity information, agencies and banks had measures in place to verify and correct missing or erroneous data prior to reporting them and officials with whom we spoke generally agreed these data were generally accurate. Based on our analysis, we concluded that the MD-715 and EEO-1 data were sufficiently reliable for our purposes.

To assess how federal financial agencies and Reserve Banks are implementing workforce diversity practices under section 342 of the Dodd-Frank Act, we reviewed agency and bank documentation of efforts to respond to the act's requirements. Sources included annual Office of Minority and Women Inclusion (OMWI) reports to Congress by agencies and banks, annual agency MD-715 reports, and other documentation provided to us by agency and bank OMWI officials. Additionally, we gathered testimonial information from agency and Reserve Bank OMWI officials on changes in the inclusion of women and minorities in their workforces and any changes in the practices used to further workforce diversity goals. Through our review of agency and Reserve Bank documentation and interviews with OMWI officials, we assessed agency and Reserve Bank efforts to measure and report on the progress of their diversity practices, as measurement was one of the nine leading diversity practices we previously identified.

To determine the extent to which agencies and Reserve Banks are implementing the requirements of the Dodd-Frank Act regarding the inclusion of women and minorities in contracting, we reviewed 2011 OMWI reports submitted to Congress and interviewed officials on their efforts in this area. We also reviewed OMWI reports to determine the dollar amount and percentage of total contracts federal financial agencies reported awarding to minority- and women-owned businesses (MWOB), and the dollar amount and percentage of total contracts Reserve Banks reporting paying MWOBs in 2011. We verified these figures and our presentation of the information with each agency and Reserve Bank, and we determined that these data were sufficiently reliable for our purposes. We interviewed agency officials on their efforts to coordinate with the Small Business Administration and other federal agencies to provide technical assistance to minority- and women-owned businesses. We collected and reviewed agency documentation of procedures developed to address the act's requirements, such as policy manuals, process workflows, and technical assistance materials. We also collected and reviewed examples of fair inclusion provisions used in agency and Reserve Bank contracts as required in section 342 of the Dodd-Frank Act.

We conducted this performance audit from January 2012 to March 2013 in accordance with generally accepted government auditing standards. Those standards require that we plan and perform the audit to obtain sufficient, appropriate evidence to provide a reasonable basis for our findings and conclusions based on our audit objectives. We believe that the evidence obtained provides a reasonable basis for our findings and conclusions based on our audit objectives.

APPENDIX II: ADDITIONAL ANALYSIS OF THE FINANCIAL SERVICES INDUSTRY

This appendix provides additional detailed analysis of EEOC data on the financial services industry by workforce position and industry sector from 2007 through 2011.

Analysis by Workforce Positions

The representation of minorities by gender was below 45 percent across all the positions throughout the same 5-year period (see fig. 16). For example, in sales positions, the representation of minorities was higher among women (about 31 percent) than among men (about 17 percent). Similarly, at the professional level, the representation of minority women was about 27 percent, compared to about 23 percent for minority men.

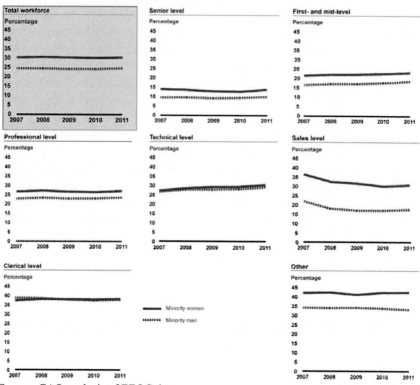

Source: GAO analysis of EEOC data.
Note: The category "other" includes craft workers, operatives, laborers, and service
workers.

Figure 16. Percentage of Minority Women and Minority Men in Various Industry
Workforce Positions in the Financial Services Industry, 2007-2011.

Analysis by Industry Sectors

Diversity remained about the same across all industry sectors in terms of
both the representation of women and minorities.[1] From 2007 through 2011,
the representation of women decreased slightly in most industry sectors and
remained below 50 percent in all sectors (see fig. 17). The "insurance carriers
and related activities" sector was the only sector that showed an increase in the
representation of women, from 47.7 percent to 48.2 percent. In contrast, the
representation of minorities increased across all sectors. Specifically, from
2007 through 2011 the representation of minorities in the "monetary

authorities-central bank" sector increased from 17 percent to 19.8 percent, and the "funds, trusts, and other financial vehicle" sector increased from 16 percent to 18.5 percent.

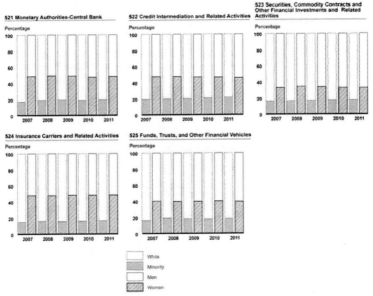

Source: GAO analysis of EEOC data.
Note: Industry sector numbers are defined as follows: Sector 521, Monetary Authorities-Central Bank; Sector 522, Credit Intermediation and Related Activities; Sector 523, Securities, Commodity Contracts, and Other Financial Investments and Related Activities; Sector 524, Insurance Carriers and Related Activities; Sector 525, Funds, Trusts, and Other Financial Vehicles.

Figure 17. Percentage of Whites/Minorities and Men/Women in Various Sectors of the Financial Services Industry, 2007-2011.

APPENDIX III: ADDITIONAL ANALYSIS OF OVERALL WORKFORCE DIVERSITY AT AGENCIES AND RESERVE BANKS

This appendix provides information accompanying our review of changes in overall workforce diversity at federal financial agencies and the 12 Reserve Banks from 2007 through 2011.[1] Tables 11 through 14 in appendix IV provide data supporting the figures in this appendix.

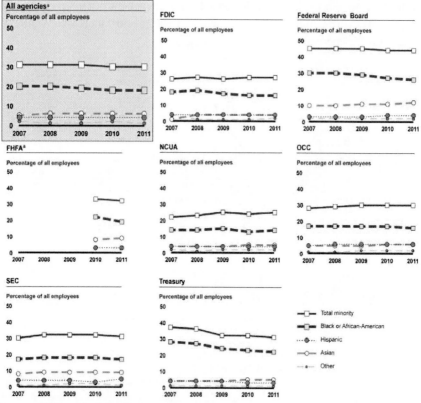

Source: GAO analysis of agency reports.

Note: Figures are rounded to the nearest percent.

For our analysis, we reviewed the numbers of employees the agencies reported according to race/ethnicity and gender in table A3 of their MD-715 reports from 2007 through 2011. These data are based on information self-reported by employees to each agency and there were some differences in reporting across the agencies. In some years, some agencies reported all employees— permanent and temporary—in their A3 tables while others reported permanent employees only.

[a]Our trend analysis for "all agencies" excludes CFPB and FHFA. CFPB assumed responsibility for certain consumer financial protection functions in July 2011 and has not yet reported workforce information to EEOC. FHFA was established in 2008 and started reporting workforce data for 2010.

Figure 18. Percentage of Minorities among All Employees at Seven Federal Financial Agencies, 2007-2011.

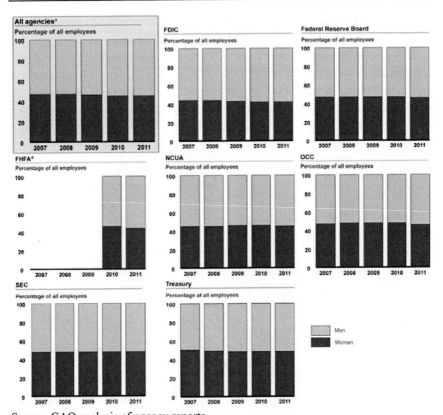

Source: GAO analysis of agency reports.

Note: Figures are rounded to the nearest percent.

For our analysis, we reviewed the numbers of employees the agencies reported according to race/ethnicity and gender in table A3 of their MD-715 reports from 2007 through 2011. These data are based on information self-reported by employees to each agency and there were some differences in reporting across the agencies. In some years, some agencies reported all employees— permanent and temporary—in their A3 tables while others reported permanent employees only.

[a]Our trend analysis for "all agencies" excludes CFPB and FHFA. CFPB assumed responsibility for certain consumer financial protection functions in July 2011 and has not yet reported workforce information to EEOC. FHFA was established in 2008 and started reporting workforce data for 2010.

Figure 19. Percentage of Women among All Employees at Seven Federal Financial Agencies, 2007-2011.

According to MD-715 data, the representation of minorities in the overall workforce of the agencies, in aggregate, changed little from 2007 through 2011. Percentage point changes in the representation of minorities at FDIC, the Federal Reserve Board, NCUA, OCC, SEC, and Treasury varied from a 5 percentage point decrease at Treasury to a 3 percentage point increase at NCUA. In 2011, the representation of minorities in the overall workforce of the agencies and FHFA ranged from 25 percent at NCUA to 44 percent at the Federal Reserve Board.

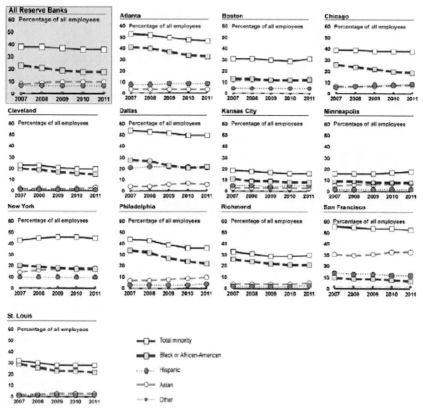

Source: GAO analysis of Federal Reserve Bank reports.
Note: Figures are rounded to the nearest percent.

Figure 20. Percentage of Minorities among All Employees at the 12 Reserve Banks, 2007-2011.

Similarly, we found that the representation of women in the overall workforce of the agencies did not change significantly from 2007 through 2011. Percentage point changes in the representation of women at the agencies from 2007 through 2011 varied from a 2 percentage point decrease at FDIC, the Federal Reserve Board, and Treasury to no percentage point change at NCUA and SEC. In 2011, the representation of minorities in the overall workforce of the agencies and FHFA ranged from 42 percent at FDIC to 48 percent at SEC and Treasury.

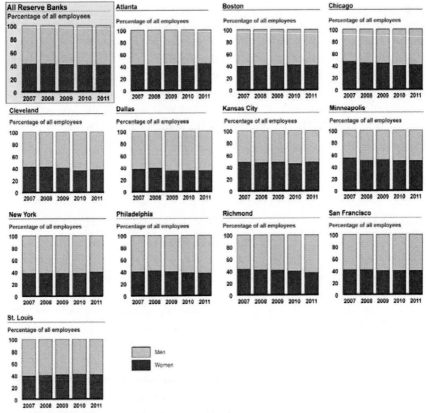

Source: GAO analysis of Federal Reserve Bank reports.
Note: Figures are rounded to the nearest percent.

Figure 21. Percentage of Women among All Employees at the 12 Reserve Banks, 2007-2011.

According to EEO-1 data provided by the Reserve Banks, the representation of minorities in the overall workforce of the Reserve Banks decreased somewhat from 2007 through 2011. The banks showed changes in the representation of minorities from 2007 through 2011, from an 8 percentage point decrease at the Reserve Bank of Philadelphia, to a 2 percentage point increase at the Reserve Banks of Minneapolis and New York. The Reserve Bank of Boston showed no percentage point change from 2007 through 2011. In 2011, the representation of minorities in the overall workforce of the Reserve Banks ranged from 16 percent at the Reserve Bank of Kansas City to 53 percent at the Reserve Bank of San Francisco.

In addition, we found that from 2007 through 2011, the representation of women in the overall workforce of the Reserve Banks also declined slightly according to EEO-1 data provided by the Reserve Banks. The Reserve Banks showed decreases in the representation of women in the overall workforce from 1 percentage point at the Reserve Bank of New York to 7 percentage points at the Reserve Bank of Cleveland. The representation of women in the overall workforce in 2011 ranged from 40 percent at the Reserve Banks of Philadelphia and Richmond to 53 percent at the Reserve Bank of Minneapolis.

APPENDIX IV: REPRESENTATION OF MINORITIES AND WOMEN AT FEDERAL FINANCIAL AGENCIES AND RESERVE BANKS

We reviewed agency and Reserve Bank reports and found that since the financial crisis, senior management-level minority and gender diversity at the agencies and Reserve Banks has varied across individual entities. We also found the representation of minorities and women in the overall workforce of the agencies changed little from 2007 through 2011, while the representation of minorities and women in the overall workforce of the Reserve Banks declined slightly. The following tables provide data supporting the senior management-level and total workforce figures in this report.

Table 7. Percentage of Minorities among Senior Management-Level Employees at Seven Federal Financial Agencies, 2007-2011

Senior management-level Reserve Bank employees (number and percent)

Race/ethnicity	Year	Atlanta		Boston		Chicago		Cleveland		Dallas		Kansas City		Minneapolis		New York		Philadelphia		Richmond		San Francisco		St. Louis	
All	2011	13	100%	13	100%	9	100%	13	100%	9	100%	12	100%	6	100%	59	100%	11	100%	22	100%	13	100%	11	100%
	2010	86	100	11	100	9	100	12	100	10	100	14	100	6	100	74	100	10	100	23	100	23	100	9	100
	2009	82	100	12	100	11	100	12	100	10	100	12	100	6	100	71	100	13	100	20	100	26	100	37	100
	2008	86	100	12	100	11	100	13	100	10	100	11	100	5	100	65	100	12	100	19	100	25	100	34	100
	2007	75	100	12	100	11	100	12	100	10	100	12	100	7	100	55	100	11	100	19	100	25	100	30	100
White	2011	10	77	11	85	8	89	13	100	8	89	11	92	5	83	52	88	10	91	19	86	10	77	10	91
	2010	72	84	11	100	8	89	12	100	9	90	13	93	5	83	66	89	9	90	20	87	20	87	9	100
	2009	68	83	12	100	10	91	12	100	9	90	12	100	5	83	62	87	11	85	19	95	23	88	33	89
	2008	72	83	12	100	10	91	13	100	9	90	11	100	5	100	55	85	10	83	17	86	23	88	31	91
	2007	62	83	12	100	10	91	12	100	9	90	12	100	6	100	46	84	10	91	18	95	24	97	29	97
Total minority	2011	3	23	2	15	1	11	0	0	1	11	1	8	1	17	7	12	1	9	3	14	3	23	1	9
	2010	14	16	0	0	1	11	0	0	1	10	1	7	1	17	8	11	1	10	3	13	3	13	0	0
	2009	14	17	0	0	1	9	0	0	1	10	0	0	1	17	9	13	2	15	1	5	3	12	4	11
	2008	14	17	0	0	1	9	0	0	1	10	0	0	1	0	10	15	2	17	2	11	3	12	3	9
	2007	13	17	0	0	1	9	0	0	1	10	0	0	1	14	9	16	1	9	1	5	2	8	1	3
Black or African American	2011	2	15	2	15	1	11	0	0	1	11	0	0	0	0	4	7	0	0	1	5	1	8	1	9
	2010	11	13	0	0	1	11	0	0	1	10	0	0	0	0	3	4	1	10	1	4	2	9	0	0
	2009	11	13	0	0	1	9	0	0	1	10	0	0	1	0	4	6	1	8	0	0	2	8	2	5
	2008	10	13	0	0	1	9	0	0	1	10	0	0	1	0	4	6	1	8	1	5	2	8	2	6
	2007	9	12	0	0	1	9	0	0	1	10	0	0	1	0	4	7	1	9	1	5	2	8	1	3
Hispanic	2011	0	0	0	0	0	0	0	0	0	0	1	8	0	0	1	1	0	0	2	0	1	8	0	0

Table 7. (Continued)

Race/ethnicity	Year	FDIC		Federal Reserve		FHFA[a]		NCUA		OCC		SEC[b]		Treasury	
		No.	%	No.	%	No.	%	No.	%	No.	%	No.	%	No.	%
	2009	7	3	5	2	-	-	5	5	6	3	-	-	12	4
	2008	5	2	4	1	-	-	5	4	9	4	-	-	8	4
	2007	4	2	3	1	-	-	4	3	6	3	-	-	5	3
Asian	2011	9	3	20	6	0	0	3	2	9	4	3	2	10	3
	2010	9	3	17	6	0	0	2	2	6	3	-	-	8	3
	2009	7	3	13	4	-	-	1	1	7	3	-	-	6	2
	2008	5	2	14	5	-	-	2	2	5	2	-	-	4	2
	2007	1	0	11	4	-	-	2	2	2	1	-	-	3	2
Other	2011	2	1	4	1	0	0	2	1	0	0	2	2	2	1
	2010	2	1	4	1	0	0	2	2	1	0	-	-	1	0
	2009	2	1	5	2	-	-	1	1	1	0	-	-	0	0
	2008	1	0	5	2	-	-	1	1	2	1	-	-	0	0
	2007	4	2	5	2	-	-	1	1	2	1	-	-	0	0

Source: GAO analysis of agency reports.

Notes: Percentages are rounded to the nearest percent.

For our analysis, we reviewed the numbers of employees the agencies reported according to race/ethnicity and gender in table A3 of their MD-715 reports from 2007 through 2011. These data are based on information self-reported by employees to each agency and there were some differences in reporting across the agencies. In some years, some agencies reported all employees—permanent and temporary—in their A3 tables while others reported permanent employees only. We considered employees reported by agencies in the category "Executive/Senior Level" as senior management-level employees. Though the MD-715 report guidelines instruct agencies to identify employees Grades 15 and above who have supervisory responsibility in this category, agencies have discretion to include employees who have significant policymaking responsibilities but do not supervise employees. As a result, the composition of the "Executive/Senior Level" category may vary among the different agencies and does not necessarily involve the same set of managers at each agency.

[a]FHFA was established in 2008 and started reporting workforce data for 2010.

[b]SEC revised how it reported officials and managers between 2007 and 2011. While our analysis includes 2011 management-level data for SEC, we excluded previous years from our trend analysis.

Table 8. Percentage of Minorities among Senior Management-Level Employees at the 12 Reserve Banks, 2007-2011

Senior management-level Reserve Bank employees (number and percent)

Race/ethnicity	Year	Atlanta		Boston		Chicago		Cleveland		Dallas		Kansas City		Minneapolis		New York		Philadelphia		Richmond		San Francisco		St. Louis	
All	2011	13	100%	13	100%	9	100%	13	100%	9	100%	12	100%	9	100%	59	100%	11	100%	22	100%	13	100%	11	100%
	2010	86	100	11	100	9	100	12	100	10	100	14	100	8	100	74	100	10	100	23	100	23	100	9	100
	2009	82	100	12	100	11	100	12	100	10	100	12	100	8	100	71	100	13	100	20	100	26	100	37	100
	2008	80	100	12	100	11	100	13	100	10	100	11	100	9	100	65	100	12	100	19	100	26	100	34	100
	2007	75	100	12	100	11	100	12	100	10	100	12	100	7	100	55	100	11	100	19	100	26	100	30	100
White	2011	10	77	11	85	8	89	13	100	8	89	11	92	5	56	52	88	10	91	19	86	10	77	10	91
	2010	72	84	11	100	8	89	12	100	9	90	13	93	5	63	66	89	9	90	20	87	20	87	9	100
	2009	68	83	12	100	10	91	12	100	9	90	12	100	7	88	62	87	11	85	19	95	23	88	33	89
	2008	66	83	12	100	10	91	13	100	9	90	11	100	8	89	55	85	10	83	17	89	23	88	31	91
	2007	62	83	12	100	10	91	12	100	9	90	12	100	6	86	46	84	10	91	18	95	24	92	29	97
Total minority	2011	3	23	2	15	1	11	0	0	1	11	1	8	4	44	7	12	1	9	3	14	3	23	1	9
	2010	14	16	0	0	1	11	0	0	1	10	1	7	3	38	8	11	1	10	3	13	3	13	0	0
	2009	14	17	0	0	1	9	0	0	1	10	0	0	1	13	9	13	2	15	1	5	3	12	4	11
	2008	14	18	0	0	1	9	0	0	1	10	0	0	1	11	10	15	2	17	2	11	3	12	3	9
	2007	13	17	0	0	1	9	0	0	1	10	0	0	1	14	9	16	1	9	1	5	2	8	1	3
Black or African American	2011	2	15	2	15	1	11	0	0	1	11	0	0	2	22	4	7	0	0	5	5	1	8	1	9
	2010	11	13	0	0	1	11	0	0	1	10	0	0	1	13	3	4	1	10	4	4	2	9	0	0
	2009	11	13	0	0	1	9	0	0	1	10	0	0	1	13	4	6	1	8	0	0	2	8	2	5
	2008	10	13	0	0	1	9	0	0	1	10	0	0	1	11	4	6	1	8	1	5	2	8	2	6
	2007	9	12	0	0	0	0	0	0	1	10	0	0	1	14	4	7	1	9	1	5	2	8	1	3
Hispanic	2011	0	0	0	0	0	0	0	0	0	0	1	8	0	0	1	2	0	0	2	9	1	8	0	0

Table 8. (Continued)

Race/ethnicity	Year	Senior management-level Reserve Bank employees (number and percent)											
		Atlanta	Boston	Chicago	Cleveland	Dallas	Kansas City	Minneapolis	New York	Philadelphia	Richmond	San Francisco	St. Louis
	2010	3	0	0	0	0	1	0	2	3	2	0	0
	2009	3	0	0	0	0	0	0	2	3	1	0	1
	2008	4	0	0	0	0	0	0	3	5	1	0	1
	2007	4	0	0	0	0	0	0	3	5	0	0	0
Asian	2011	0	0	0	0	0	0	11	2	9	0	8	0
	2010	0	0	0	0	0	0	13	3	4	0	4	0
	2009	0	0	0	0	0	0	0	3	4	0	4	0
	2008	0	0	0	0	0	0	0	3	5	0	4	0
	2007	0	0	0	0	0	0	0	2	4	0	0	0
Other	2011	1	0	0	0	0	0	11	0	0	0	0	0
	2010	0	0	0	0	0	0	13	0	0	0	0	0
	2009	0	0	0	0	0	0	0	0	0	0	0	0
	2008	0	0	0	0	0	0	0	0	0	0	0	0
	2007	0	0	0	0	0	0	0	0	0	0	0	0

Source: GAO analysis of EEO-1 reports provided by Reserve Banks.

Notes: Percentages are rounded to the nearest percent.

For our analysis of the representation of minorities and women at the senior management level for Reserve Banks, we reviewed the numbers of employees the banks reported as "Executive/Senior Level Officials and Managers" from 2007 through 2011. While EEOC provides instructions on reporting job categories based on the skill levels, knowledge, and responsibilities involved in occupations identified within each job category, employers have discretion to decide which positions they report as Executive/Senior Level Officials and Managers versus those at lower levels of management. Therefore, comparisons of a given management level between the Reserve Banks do not necessarily involve the same set of managers at each bank. For example, the Reserve Bank of Atlanta revised how it reported officials and managers for 2011. From 2007 through 2010, the bank reported all officers as Executive/Senior Level Officials and Managers, and for 2011, the bank reported as Executive/Senior Level Officials and Managers those employees that have strategic roles and/or report to the Reserve Bank's President. According to Reserve Bank officials, recent efforts have been made to align reporting of officials and managers across the Federal Reserve System.

Table 9. Percentage of Women among Senior Management-Level Employees at Seven Federal Financial Agencies, 2007-2011

Senior management-level federal financial agency employees (number and percent)

Gender	Year	FDIC		Federal Reserve		FHFA[a]		NCUA		OCC		SEC[b]		Treasury	
All	2011	301	100%	343	100%	51	100%	134	100%	261	100%	125	100%	312	100%
	2010	284	100	307	100	29	100	109	100	204	100	-	-	279	100
	2009	257	100	301	100	-	-	101	100	201	100	-	-	176	100
	2008	234	100	289	100	-	-	123	100	252	100	-	-	219	100
	2007	203	100	253	100	-	-	118	100	229	100	-	-	175	100
Men	2011	209	69	201	59	27	53	87	65	171	68	85	68	192	62
	2010	197	69	185	60	14	48	77	71	137	67	-	-	178	64
	2009	187	72	184	61	-	-	72	71	130	65	-	-	176	64
	2008	165	71	180	62	-	-	84	68	161	64	-	-	143	65
	2007	147	72	155	61	-	-	82	69	145	63	-	-	115	66
Women	2011	92	31	142	41	24	47	47	35	80	32	40	32	120	38
	2010	87	31	122	40	15	52	32	29	67	33	-	-	101	36
	2009	71	28	117	39	-	-	29	29	71	35	-	-	100	36
	2008	69	29	109	38	-	-	39	32	91	36	-	-	76	35
	2007	56	28	98	39	-	-	36	31	84	37	-	-	60	34

Source: GAO analysis of agency reports.

Notes: Percentages are rounded to the nearest percent.

For our analysis, we reviewed the numbers of employees the agencies reported according to race/ethnicity and gender in table A3 of their MD-715 reports from 2007 through 2011. These data are based on information self-reported by employees to each agency and there were some differences in reporting across the agencies. In some years, some agencies reported all employees— permanent and temporary—in their A3 tables while others reported permanent employees only. We considered employees reported by agencies in the category "Executive/Senior Level" as senior management-level employees. Though the MD-715 report guidelines instruct agencies to identify employees Grades 15 and above who have supervisory responsibility in this category, agencies have discretion to include employees who have significant policymaking responsibilities but do not supervise employees. As a result, the composition of the "Executive/Senior Level" category may vary among the different agencies and does not necessarily involve the same set of managers at each agency.

[a] FHFA was established in 2008 and started reporting workforce data for 2010.

[b] SEC revised how it reported officials and managers between 2007 and 2011. While our analysis includes 2011 management-level data for SEC, we excluded previous years from our trend analysis.

Table 10. Percentage of Women among Senior Management-Level Employees at the 12 Reserve Banks, 2007-2011

Race/ ethnicity	Year	Atlanta		Boston		Chicago		Cleveland		Dallas		Kansas City		Minneapolis		New York		Philadelphia		Richmond		San Francisco		St. Louis	
		— Senior management-level federal financial agency employees (number and percent)																							
All	2011	13	100%	13	100%	9	100%	13	100%	9	100%	12	100%	9	100%	59	100%	11	100%	22	100%	13	100%	11	100%
	2010	86	100	11	100	9	100	12	100	10	100	14	100	8	100	74	100	10	100	23	100	23	100	9	100
	2009	82	100	12	100	11	100	12	100	10	100	11	100	8	100	71	100	13	100	20	100	26	100	37	100
	2008	80	100	12	100	11	100	13	100	10	100	11	100	9	100	65	100	12	100	19	100	26	100	54	100
	2007	75	100	12	100	11	100	12	100	10	100	12	100	7	100	55	100	11	100	19	100	26	100	30	100
Men	2011	7	54	11	85	5	56	9	69	6	67	5	42	6	67	34	58	6	55	15	68	9	69	7	64
	2010	53	62	9	82	5	56	9	75	7	70	9	64	6	75	46	65	6	50	16	70	16	70	6	67
	2009	49	60	9	75	6	55	8	67	7	70	8	67	6	75	46	65	9	69	13	65	17	65	26	70
	2008	49	61	9	75	6	55	9	69	7	70	8	73	7	78	43	66	8	67	14	74	17	65	22	65
	2007	48	64	11	75	6	55	8	67	7	70	8	67	6	86	39	71	7	64	15	79	17	65	20	67
Women	2011	6	46	2	15	4	44	4	31	3	33	7	58	3	33	25	42	5	45	7	32	4	31	4	36
	2010	33	38	2	18	4	44	3	25	3	30	5	36	2	25	26	36	5	50	7	30	7	30	3	33
	2009	33	40	3	25	5	45	4	33	3	30	4	33	2	25	25	35	4	31	7	35	9	35	11	30
	2008	31	39	3	25	5	45	4	31	3	30	3	27	2	22	22	34	4	33	5	26	9	35	12	35
	2007	27	36	3	25	5	45	4	33	3	30		33	1	14	16	29	4	36	4	21	9	35	10	33

Source: GAO analysis of EEO-1 reports provided by Reserve Banks. Notes: Percentages are rounded to the nearest percent.

For our analysis of the representation of minorities and women at the senior management level for Reserve Banks, we reviewed the numbers of employees the banks reported as "Executive/Senior Level Officials and Managers" from 2007 through 2011. While EEOC provides instructions on reporting job categories based on the skill levels, knowledge, and responsibilities involved in occupations identified within each job category, employers have discretion to decide which positions they report as Executive/Senior Level Officials and Managers versus those at lower levels of management. Therefore, comparisons of a given management level between the Reserve Banks do not necessarily involve the same set of managers at each bank. For example, the Reserve Bank of Atlanta revised how it reported officials and managers for 2011. From 2007 through 2010, the bank reported all officers as Executive/Senior Level Officials and Managers, and for 2011, the bank reported as Executive/Senior Level Officials and Managers those employees that have strategic roles and/or report to the Reserve Bank's President. According to Reserve Bank officials, recent efforts have been made to align reporting of officials and managers across the Federal Reserve System.

Table 11. Percentage of Minorities among All Employees at Seven Federal Financial Agencies, 2007-2011

Race/ethnicity	Year	FDIC		Federal Reserve		FHFA[a]		NCUA		OCC		SEC		Treasury	
							Federal financial agency employees (number and percent)								
All	2011	8,398	100%	2,274	100%	494	100%	1,159	100%	3,560	100%	3,812	100%	1,586	100%
	2010	8,316	100	2,137	100	406	100	1,095	100	3,054	100	3,897	100	1,599	100
	2009	6,530	100	2,143	100	-	-	1,074	100	3,117	100	3,720	100	1,599	100
	2008	5,028	100	2,028	100	-	-	934	100	3,039	100	3,653	100	1,295	100
	2007	4,428	100	1,945	100	-	-	929	100	3,000	100	3,154	100	1,223	100
White	2011	6,152	73	1,276	56	335	38	871	75	2,503	70	2,616	69	1,087	69
	2010	6,107	73	1,196	56	270	67	833	76	2,145	70	2,664	68	1,080	68
	2009	4,800	74	1,187	55	-	-	769	75	2,185	70	2,516	68	1,041	68
	2008	3,655	73	1,115	55	-	-	722	78	2,161	72	2,204	70	772	63
	2007	3,261	74	1,066	55	-	-	722	78	2,161	72	2,204	7	772	63
Total minority	2011	2,246	27	998	44	159	32	288	25	1,057	30	1,196	31	499	31
	2010	2,209	27	941	44	136	33	262	24	909	30	1,233	32	519	32
	2009	1,730	26	956	45	-	-	255	25	932	30	1,204	32	488	32
	2008	1,373	27	913	45	-	-	216	23	887	29	1,168	32	464	36
	2007	1,167	26	879	45	-	-	207	22	839	28	950	30	451	37
Black or African American	2011	1,385	16	591	26	95	19	157	14	577	16	632	17	356	22
	2010	1,353	16	582	27	90	22	141	13	508	17	682	18	372	23
	2009	1,109	17	612	29	-	-	153	15	534	17	679	18	362	24
	2008	944	19	604	30	-	-	133	14	517	17	668	18	352	27
	2007	799	18	589	30	-	-	126	14	501	17	523	17	344	28
Hispanic	2011	359	4	94	4	17	3	48	4	201	6	182	5	46	3
	2010	364	4	81	4	12	3	47	4	181	6	133	3	49	3

Table 11. (Continued)

Race/ethnicity	Year	Federal financial agency employees (number and percent)													
		FDIC		Federal Reserve		FHFA[a]		NCUA		OCC		SEC		Treasury	
	2009	261	4	75	3	-	-	43	4	181	6	144	4	54	4
	2008	198	4	70	3	-	-	35	4	168	6	137	4	47	4
	2007	181	4	68	3	-	-	34	4	157	5	129	4	50	4
Asian	2011	374	4	271	12	46	9	56	5	212	6	354	9	80	5
	2010	372	4	238	11	33	8	52	5	169	6	352	9	79	5
	2009	283	4	231	11	-	-	37	4	163	5	319	9	60	4
	2008	199	4	204	10	-	-	36	4	158	5	312	9	53	4
	2007	25	1	187	10	-	-	33	4	145	5	266	8	49	4
Other	2011	128	2	42	2	1	0	27	2	67	2	28	1	17	1
	2010	120	1	40	2	1	0	22	2	51	2	66	2	19	1
	2009	77	1	38	2	-	-	22	2	54	2	62	2	12	1
	2008	32	1	35	2	-	-	12	1	44	1	51	1	12	1
	2007	162	4	35	2	-	-	14	2	36	1	32	1	8	1

Source: GAO analysis of agency reports.

Notes: Percentages are rounded to the nearest percent.

For our analysis, we reviewed the numbers of employees the agencies reported according to race/ethnicity and gender in table A3 of their MD–715 reports from 2007 through 2011. These data are based on information self-reported by employees to each agency and there were some differences in reporting across the agencies. In some years, some agencies reported all employees—permanent and temporary—in their A3 tables while others reported permanent employees only.

[a] FHFA was established in 2008 and started reporting workforce data for 2010.

Table 12. Percentage of Minorities among All Employees at the 12 Reserve Banks, 2007-2011

Reserve Bank employees (number and percent)

Race/ethnicity	Year	Atlanta		Boston		Chicago		Cleveland		Dallas		Kansas City		Minneapolis		New York		Philadelphia		Richmond		San Francisco		St. Louis	
All	2011	1,594	100%	875	100%	1,431	100%	1,094	100%	1,098	100%	1,225	100%	1,011	100%	2,955	100%	839	100%	2,444	100%	1,495	100%	955	100%
	2010	1,623	100	858	100	1,353	100	1,276	100	1,110	100	1,292	100	1,004	100	2,999	100	840	100	2,356	100	1,574	100	944	100
	2009	1,728	100	868	100	1,379	100	1,340	100	1,168	100	1,220	100	1,051	100	2,940	100	914	100	2,421	100	1,632	100	932	100
	2008	1,886	100	884	100	1,415	100	1,511	100	1,225	100	1,277	100	1,172	100	2,791	100	1,016	100	2,534	100	1,700	100	987	100
	2007	2,017	100	978	100	1,532	100	1,568	100	1,269	100	1,357	100	1,278	100	2,860	100	1,092	100	2,733	100	1,779	100	1,089	100
White	2011	839	53	607	69	889	62	878	80	551	50	1,026	84	830	82	1,617	55	539	64	1,721	70	701	47	691	72
	2010	839	52	607	71	845	62	1,017	80	555	50	1,082	84	830	83	1,626	54	534	64	1,672	71	703	46	679	72
	2009	864	50	611	70	850	62	1,063	79	561	48	1,018	83	879	84	1,596	54	562	61	1,719	71	758	46	674	72
	2008	899	48	614	69	866	61	1,168	77	572	47	1,050	82	980	84	1,522	55	581	57	1,753	69	768	45	694	70
	2007	949	47	676	69	933	61	1,213	77	590	46	1,096	81	1,071	84	1,630	57	613	56	1,823	67	774	44	740	68
Total minority	2011	755	47	268	31	542	38	216	20	547	50	199	16	181	18	1,338	45	300	36	722	30	794	53	264	28
	2010	784	48	251	29	508	38	259	20	555	50	210	16	174	17	1,373	46	306	36	684	29	811	54	265	28
	2009	864	50	257	30	529	38	277	21	607	52	202	17	172	16	1,344	46	352	39	702	29	874	54	258	28
	2008	987	52	270	31	549	39	343	23	653	53	227	18	192	16	1,269	45	435	43	781	31	932	55	293	30
	2007	1068	53	302	31	599	39	355	23	679	54	261	19	207	16	1,230	43	479	44	910	33	1,005	56	349	32
Black or African American	2011	525	33	108	12	279	19	167	15	238	22	93	8	79	8	494	17	184	22	509	21	101	7	209	22
	2010	557	34	106	12	275	20	208	16	229	21	107	8	81	8	523	17	198	24	503	21	116	8	215	23
	2009	634	37	107	12	310	22	228	17	269	23	109	9	82	8	530	18	248	27	533	22	140	9	216	23
	2008	758	40	117	13	334	24	290	19	326	27	120	9	102	9	539	19	330	32	603	24	160	9	254	26
	2007	830	41	132	13	391	26	308	20	354	28	146	11	118	9	560	20	372	34	713	26	178	10	315	29
Hispanic	2011	147	9	45	5	132	9	12	1	235	21	57	5	24	2	301	10	31	4	65	3	179	12	19	2

Table 12. (Continued)

Race/ethnicity	Year	Atlanta		Boston		Chicago		Cleveland		Dallas		Kansas City		Minneapolis		New York		Philadelphia		Richmond		San Francisco		St. Louis	
		Reserve Bank employees (number and percent)																							
	2010	148	9	41	5	114	8	13	1	247	22	59	5	21	2	301	10	28	3	58	2	177	12	19	2
	2009	162	9	44	5	112	8	13	1	260	22	61	4	20	2	290	10	28	3	65	2	206	13	15	2
	2008	148	8	47	5	102	7	16	1	265	22	62	5	20	2	278	10	28	3	59	2	224	13	15	2
	2007	153	8	52	5	96	6	14	1	266	21	67	5	20	2	260	10	29	3	63	2	251	14	9	1
Asian	2011	69	4	112	13	119	8	29	3	67	6	41	3	71	7	523	18	80	10	129	5	490	33	33	3
	2010	68	4	104	12	109	8	31	2	73	7	40	3	66	7	532	18	76	9	103	4	493	33	29	3
	2009	68	4	105	12	95	7	29	2	70	6	38	3	64	6	508	17	73	8	96	4	502	31	25	3
	2008	72	4	106	12	101	7	28	2	54	4	41	3	65	6	439	16	75	7	103	4	516	30	22	2
	2007	78	4	117	12	104	7	26	2	53	4	43	3	64	5	389	14	75	7	113	4	547	31	23	2
Other	2011	14	1	3	0	12	1	8	1	7	1	8	1	7	1	20	1	5	1	20	1	24	1	2	0
	2010	11	1	0	0	10	1	7	1	6	1	4	0	6	1	17	1	5	1	23	1	25	2	2	0
	2009	10	1	1	0	12	1	7	1	8	1	4	0	6	0	16	1	3	0	17	1	27	2	2	0
	2008	9	0	0	0	12	1	9	1	8	1	4	0	5	0	13	0	2	0	15	1	32	2	2	0
	2007	7	0	1	0	8	1	7	0	6	0	5	0	5	0	1	0	3	0	21	1	29	2	2	0

Source: GAO analysis of EEO-1 reports provided by Reserve Banks.

Note: Percentages are rounded to the nearest percent.

Table 13. Percentage of Women among All Employees at Seven Federal Financial Agencies, 2007-2011

Gender	Year	Federal financial agency employees (number and percent)													
		FDIC		Federal Reserve		FHFA[a]		NCUA		OCC		SEC		Treasury	
All	2011	8,398	100%	2,274	100%	494	100%	1,159	100%	3,560	100%	3,812	100%	1,586	100%
	2010	8,316	100	2,137	100	406	100	1,095	100	3,054	100	3,897	100	1,599	100
	2009	6,530	100	2,143	100	-	-	1,024	100	3,117	100	3,720	100	1,529	100
	2008	5,028	100	2,028	100	-	-	934	100	3,039	100	3,653	100	1,295	100
	2007	4,428	100	1,945	100	-	-	929	100	3,000	100	3,154	100	1,223	100
Men	2011	4,846	58	1,238	54	277	56	640	55	1,917	54	1,984	52	822	52
	2010	4,852	58	1,138	53	219	54	589	54	1,587	52	2,024	52	827	52
	2009	3,735	57	1,140	53	-	-	555	54	1,617	52	1,924	52	798	52
	2008	2,809	56	1,080	53	-	-	515	55	1,584	52	1,882	52	657	51
	2007	2,462	56	1,022	53	-	-	509	55	1,583	53	1,655	52	613	50
Women	2011	3,552	42	1,036	46	217	44	519	45	1,643	46	1,828	48	764	48
	2010	3,464	42	999	47	187	46	506	46	1,467	48	1,873	48	772	48
	2009	2,795	43	1,003	47	-	-	469	46	1,500	48	1,796	48	731	48
	2008	2,219	44	948	47	-	-	419	45	1,455	48	1,771	48	638	49
	2007	1,966	44	923	47	-	-	420	45	1,417	47	1,499	48	610	50

Source: GAO analysis of agency reports.

Note: Percentages are rounded to the nearest percent.

For our analysis, we reviewed the numbers of employees the agencies reported according to race/ethnicity and gender in table A3 of their MD-715 reports from 2007 through 2011. These data are based on information self-reported by employees to each agency and there were some differences in reporting across the agencies. In some years, some agencies reported all employees—permanent and temporary—in their A3 tables while others reported permanent employees only.

[a] FHFA was established in 2008 and started reporting workforce data for 2010.

Table 14. Percentage of Women among All Employees at the 12 Reserve Banks, 2007-2011

Reserve Bank employees (number and percent)

Racial/Ethnicity	Year	Atlanta		Boston		Chicago		Cleveland		Dallas		Kansas City		Minneapolis		New York		Philadelphia		Richmond		San Francisco		St. Louis	
All	2011	1,594	100%	875	100%	1,431	100%	1,094	100%	1,098	100%	1,225	100%	1,011	100%	2,965	100%	869	100%	2,444	100%	1,495	100%	955	100%
	2010	1,623	100	858	100	1,353	100	1,276	100	1,110	100	1,292	100	1,004	100	2,999	100	840	100	2,366	100	1,514	100	944	100
	2009	1,728	100	868	100	1,379	100	1,340	100	1,168	100	1,220	100	1,051	100	2,940	100	914	100	2,421	100	1,632	100	932	100
	2008	1,886	100	884	100	1,415	100	1,511	100	1,225	100	1,277	100	1,172	100	2,791	100	1016	100	2,534	100	1,700	100	987	100
	2007	2,017	100	978	100	1,532	100	1,568	100	1,269	100	1,357	100	1,278	100	2,860	100	1062	100	2,733	100	1,779	100	1,089	100
Men	2011	863	54	475	54	775	54	594	54	631	57	650	53	473	47	1,587	54	503	60	1,460	60	889	59	517	54
	2010	866	53	469	55	728	54	648	51	640	58	677	52	468	47	1,621	54	498	59	1,396	59	905	60	510	54
	2009	913	53	471	54	729	53	678	51	669	57	617	51	474	45	1,600	54	492	58	1,410	58	950	58	499	54
	2008	964	51	477	54	707	50	727	48	685	56	626	49	497	42	1,506	54	567	56	1,420	56	959	56	526	53
	2007	1,008	50	491	50	745	49	741	47	669	54	647	48	521	41	1,512	53	603	55	1,505	55	992	56	556	51
Women	2011	741	46	400	46	656	46	500	46	467	43	575	47	538	53	1,368	46	336	40	984	40	606	41	438	46
	2010	707	47	389	45	625	46	620	49	470	42	615	48	536	53	1,370	46	342	41	960	41	609	40	434	46
	2009	815	47	397	46	650	47	662	49	499	43	603	49	577	55	1,340	46	352	42	1,011	42	682	42	433	46
	2008	922	49	407	46	708	50	784	52	540	44	651	51	675	58	1,285	46	449	44	1,114	44	741	44	461	47
	2007	1,009	50	487	50	787	51	827	53	580	46	710	52	757	59	1,348	47	489	45	1,228	45	787	44	533	49

Source: GAO analysis of EEO-1 reports provided by Reserve Banks.

Note: Percentages are rounded to the nearest percent.

End Notes

[1] GAO has conducted prior work on the challenges faced in the financial sector for promoting and retaining a diverse workforce. See GAO, *Financial Services Industry: Overall Trends in Management-Level Diversity and Diversity Initiatives, 1993-2004*, GAO-06-617 (Washington, D.C.: June 1, 2006) and *Financial Services Industry: Overall Trends in Management-Level Diversity and Diversity Initiatives, 1993-2008*, GAO-10-736T (Washington, D.C.: May 12, 2010).

[2] Pub. L. No. 111-203 § 342,124 Stat.1376,1441-1443 (2010).The federal agencies required to meet the workforce diversity provisions in section 342 of the Dodd-Frank Act include the Departmental Offices of the Department of the Treasury (Treasury), the Federal Deposit Insurance Corporation (FDIC), the Federal Housing Finance Agency (FHFA), the Board of Governors of the Federal Reserve System (Federal Reserve Board), the National Credit Union Administration (NCUA), the Office of the Comptroller of the Currency (OCC), the Securities and Exchange Commission (SEC), and the Bureau of Consumer Financial Protection, commonly known as the Consumer Financial Protection Bureau (CFPB). Throughout the report we refer to these as either federal financial agencies or agencies.

[3] CFPB had until January 21, 2012, to establish its OMWI and begin addressing the other requirements of the act.

[4] The race/ethnicity categories in EEOC data include White, Black, Hispanic, Asian, and other races. All non-White categories in EEOC data are considered racial/ethnic minorities in this report.

[5] See GAO-06-617 and GAO-10-736T.

[6] GAO, *Diversity Management: Expert-Identified Leading Practices and Agency Examples*, GAO-05-90 (Washington, D.C.: Jan. 14, 2005).

[7] Pub. L. No. 111-203. § 342, 124 Stat. 1376, 1541-1544 (2010). CFPB had until January 21, 2012, to comply with the requirements.

[8] Federal Reserve Act, 63 Cong. Ch. 6, 38 Stat. 251-275 (Dec. 23, 1913).

[9] For purposes of the act, minority means any Black American, Native American, Hispanic American, or Asian American. Minority-owned business means a business (i) more than 50 percent of the ownership or control of which is held by one or more minority individuals; and (ii) more than 50 percent of net profit and loss of which accrues to one or more minority individuals. Women-owned business means a business (i) more than 50 percent of the ownership or control of which is held by one or more women; (ii) more than 50 percent of the new profit or loss of which accrues to one or more women; and (iii) a significant percentage of senior management positions are held by women.

[10] Section 342 applies to all contracts of an agency for services of any kind, including the services of financial institutions, investment-banking firms, mortgage banking entities, underwriters, accountants, investment consultants, and providers of legal services. It also includes all contracts for all business and activities of an agency, at all levels, including contracts for the issuance or guarantee of any debt, equity, or security; the sale of assets; the management of assets of the agency; the making of equity investments by the agency; and the implementation of programs to address economic recovery.

[11] EEOC compiles EEO-1 data from the reports it collects annually from private employers with 100 or more employees or federal contractors with 50 or more employees. Similar to our 2006 report, we obtained data from EEOC for private employers with 100 or more employees. Consequently, the analysis included in this report may not match the analysis found in EEOC's website, which would also include federal contractors with 50 or more

employees. The financial services industry EEO-1 data analysis provided in this section of the report includes workforce information from the 12 Federal Reserve Banks, as they are considered part of the financial services industry. We provide a separate analysis of the 12 Federal Reserve Banks' workforce later in the report because they were also covered by the Dodd-Frank Act provisions.

[12] GAO-06-617. The representation of minorities varied among management positions, which EEOC splits into two categories: (1) first- and mid-level officials and managers and (2) senior-level officials and managers. In 2011, the representation of minorities among first- and mid-level managers stood at 20.4 percent, about 1 percentage point higher to the representation of minorities among all management positions, according to EEOC data (see fig. 2). In contrast, at the senior management level, representation of minorities was 10.8 percent in 2011, about 8 percentage points below their representation among all management positions; yet representation of minorities in first- and mid-level management positions consistently increased from 18.7 percent to 20.4 percent over the 5-year period. First- and mid-level management positions may serve as an internal pipeline in an organization through which minority candidates could move into senior management positions.

[13] GAO-06-617.

[14] We determined the CPS-estimated minority percentages of management positions within the financial services industry cannot be precisely measured. However, CPS-estimated minority percentages were included in this report to provide some more context. Since many of the percentage estimates have wide confidence intervals, we encourage the reader to interpret the CPS-estimated minority percentages in this report with caution. Please see appendix I for the estimated minority percentages and standard errors.

[15] As previously discussed the nine leading diversity practices are (1) commitment to diversity as demonstrated and communicated by an organization's top leadership; (2) the inclusion of diversity management in an organization's strategic plan; (3) diversity linked to performance, making the case that a more diverse and inclusive work environment could help improve productivity and individual and organizational performance; (4) measurement of the impact of various aspects of a diversity program; (5) management accountability for the progress of diversity initiatives; (6) succession planning; (7) recruitment; (8) employee involvement in an organization's diversity management; and (9) training for management and staff about diversity management. See GAO-05-90.

[16] This relates to leading practice diversity linked to performance, which refers to the understanding that a more diverse and inclusive work environment can yield greater productivity and help improve individuals' and organization performance, while employee involvement refers to the contribution of employees in driving diversity throughout an organization. See GAO-05-90.

[17] GAO-06-617 and GAO-10-736T.

[18] GAO-06-617.

[19] GAO-06-617 and GAO-10-736T.

[20] GAO-06-617 and GAO-10-736T.

[21] We refer to overall representation of students from undergraduate, graduate, and doctoral programs as the university system. These data exclude specialized graduate programs, such as Master of Economics. In addition, these overall percentages only represent enrolled students for which race/ethnicity or gender were indicated.

[22] AACSB, the world's largest accreditation association for business schools, conducts an annual survey called "Business School Questionnaire" of all its member schools. Participation in this survey is voluntary.

[23] Accountability refers to the means to ensure that leaders are responsible for diversity by aligning their performance assessment and compensation to the progress of diversity initiatives. See GAO-05-90.

[24] Our analysis of employment data in this section of the report differs from how EEOC typically reports data. While EEOC reports on individual equal employment opportunity groups, we report on minorities as a group. Additional data and figures supporting this section of the report are in appendixes III and IV.

[25] On July 21, 2010, the Consumer Financial Protection Act established CFPB as an independent bureau within the Federal Reserve System to be headed by a director. Effective July 21, 2011, CFPB assumed responsibility for certain consumer financial protection functions formerly the responsibilities of the Board of Governors of the Federal Reserve System, the Comptroller of the Currency, the Director of the Office of Thrift Supervision, FDIC, the Federal Trade Commission, NCUA, and the Secretary of the Department of Housing and Urban Development.

[26] CFPB provided to us workforce diversity data for all employees, senior officials, and supervisors as of May 19, 2012.

[27] Federal financial agencies provided us reports they issued according to EEOC Management Directive 715, known as MD-715 reports. This directive does not apply to the Federal Reserve Banks, as they are not federal agencies. Our analysis of the representation of minorities and women at the senior management level for agencies reviewed the numbers of employees the agencies reported as "Executive/Senior Level" from 2007 through 2011. Though the MD-715 reports allow for this category to cover Grades 15 and above, agencies have discretion to decide which positions are included in this senior level versus those the agencies include at lower levels of management. Therefore, comparisons of a given management level between the agencies do not necessarily involve the same set of managers at each agency. Figures in our analysis are rounded to the nearest percent.

[28] Percentage changes in the representation of minorities among senior management-level employees from 2007 through 2011 for NCUA and OCC were zero when rounded to the nearest percent. The representation of minorities among senior management-level employees was 12 percent at NCUA in 2007 and 2011, and at OCC, 17 percent in 2007 and 18 percent in 2011.

[29] CFPB identified these employees as Executive/Senior Officials.

[30] Reserve Banks provided us reports they issued to EEOC according to form EEO-1. Our analysis of senior management-level representation for the Reserve Banks included employees the banks reported as "Executive/Senior Officials and Managers." Figures in our analysis are rounded to the nearest percent.

[31] Among other things, the act outlines steps the specific agencies and Reserve Banks should take to seek workforce diversity at all levels of their organizations. These steps include recruiting from colleges serving primarily minority populations, sponsoring and recruiting at job fairs in urban communities, and advertising positions in newspapers and magazines oriented toward minorities and women.

[32] SEC determined it could not use appropriated funds for the purpose of establishing an OMWI without first obtaining congressional approval. Its reprogramming request was approved by the House and Senate Appropriations Committees in July 2011.

[33] As mentioned previously, on July 21, 2010, the Consumer Financial Protection Act of 2010 established CFPB as an independent bureau within the Federal Reserve System to be headed by a director. Effective July 21, 2011, CFPB assumed responsibility for certain consumer financial protection functions formerly the responsibilities of the Board of Governors of the Federal Reserve System, the Comptroller of the Currency, the Director of the Office of Thrift Supervision, FDIC, the Federal Trade Commission, NCUA, and the Secretary of the Department of Housing and Urban Development. CFPB had until January 21, 2012, to establish its OMWI and begin addressing the other requirements of the act.

[34] Pub. L. No. 111-203. § 342(b)(2) (2010).

[35] Exec. Order 13583 (2011).

[36] Although this report reviews eight federal agencies, this requirement does not apply to Treasury Departmental Offices, as the agency does not have regulated entities. Additionally, the requirement does not directly apply to the Reserve Banks. However, the Federal Reserve Board has delegated some of its supervisory responsibilities to the Reserve Banks—such as responsibility for examining bank and thrift holding companies and state member banks under rules, regulations, and policies established by the Federal Reserve Board. The scope of these delegated authorities does not include section 342 oversight of regulated entities at this time.

[37] Pub. L. No. 110-289 § 1116, 122 Stat. 2654, 2681-2683 (2008). Under HERA, FHFA's regulated entities must establish an OMWI and develop and implement standards and procedures to ensure, to the maximum extent possible, the inclusion and utilization of minorities and women, and minority- and women-owned businesses in all business and activities of the regulated entity at all levels, including in procurement, insurance, and all types of contracts. Additionally, each of its regulated entities must report annually to FHFA on actions taken pursuant to these requirements. Further, the act requires FHFA to take affirmative steps to seek diversity in its workforce at all levels, consistent with the demographic diversity of the United States.

[38] Minority and Women Inclusion. 12 C.F.R. § 1207.1 -24 (Dec. 28, 2010).

[39] Pub. L. No. 111-203. § 342(b)(4) (2010). Even though section 342 provides for the development of standards for the assessment of diversity policies and practices of regulated entities, it further provides that nothing in the requirement may be construed to require any specific action based on the findings of the assessment.

[40] 5 U.S.C. § 552. The Freedom of Information Act requires that federal agencies provide the public with access to government records and information on the basis of the principles of openness and accountability in government.

[41] Pub. L. No. 111-203, § 342(e)(5) (2010).

[42] GAO-05-90.

[43] For purposes of the act, minority-owned business means a business for which more than 50 percent of the ownership is held by one or more minority individuals and more than 50 percent of net profit and loss of the business accrues to one or more minority individuals. Women-owned business means a business for which more than 50 percent of the ownership is held by one or more women, more than 50 percent of the net profit or loss of the business accrues to one or more women, and a significant percentage of senior management positions are held by women.

[44] The FAR is the primary regulation for use by all federal executive agencies in their acquisition of supplies and services with appropriated funds. Two federal financial agencies subject to the contracting provisions in section 342 of Dodd-Frank are also governed by the FAR because they receive appropriated funds: SEC and Treasury. The other agencies included in

this report are not legally required to follow the FAR because they do not receive appropriated funds. However, according to CFPB, FDIC, FHFA, and OCC these agencies choose to adhere to part or all of this regulation. According to NCUA, it used the FAR as guidance when establishing its contracting procedures. The Federal Reserve Board described their procurement policy as consistent with the FAR.

[45] As previously discussed, the Reserve Banks are not federal agencies.

[46] According to one Reserve Bank, there are certain types of contracts from which the fair inclusion provision would be automatically excluded. For example, the Reserve Bank of Chicago would not include the provision in a new contract with a vendor that has an existing contract with the National Procurement Office of the Federal Reserve System because in that previous contract the vendor had already agreed to make efforts to include women and minorities in its workforce.

[47] The Office of Federal Contract Compliance Programs enforces, for the benefit of job seekers and wage earners, the contractual promise of affirmative action and equal employment opportunity required of those who do business with the federal government.

[48] The act does not set a standard that the federal agencies or Reserve Banks must meet in making contracting awards to MWOBs.

[49] The Small Business Administration (SBA) negotiates goals with federal agencies for contract dollars awarded to small businesses to meet statutory government-wide goals. 15 U.S.C. § 664(g) sets forth a statutory goal for 23 percent of all aggregated federal contracting dollars to be awarded to small businesses. These include current goals for 5 percent of all prime contract and subcontract dollars to be awarded to small disadvantaged businesses and 5 percent of all prime contract and subcontract dollars to be awarded to women-owned small businesses. SBA also negotiates goals for the award of contract dollars to service-disabled veteran-owned and HUBZone small businesses.

[50] See GAO, *Government Contracts: Federal Efforts to Assist Small Minority Owned Businesses*, GAO-12-873 (Washington, D.C.: Sept. 28, 2012). We analyzed data from the Federal Procurement Data System—Next Generation. Minority designations are self-reported, and some businesses are both minority- and women-owned and may be counted under both categories.

[51] The NPO, housed in the Reserve Bank of Richmond, conducts research and negotiates, manages, and administers contracts on behalf of the 12 Reserve Banks, but the purchases are made by the individual Reserve Bank that chooses to use the contract.

[52] A mentor-protégé program is an arrangement in which mentors—businesses, typically experienced prime contractors—provide technical, managerial, and other business development assistance to eligible small businesses, or protégés. Overall, mentor-protégé programs seek to enhance the ability of small businesses to compete more successfully for federal government contracts by furnishing them with assistance to improve their performance. See GAO, *Mentor-Protégé Programs Have Policies that Aim to Benefit Participants but Do Not Require Postagreement Tracking*, GAO-11-548R (Washington, D.C.: June 15, 2011) and *Small Business Contracting: Opportunities to Improve the Effectiveness of Agency and SBA Advocates and Mentor-Protégé Programs*, GAO-11-844T (Washington, D.C.: Sept. 15, 2011).

End Notes for Appendix I

[1] Federal contractors with 50 or more employees are also required to submit to EEOC annual reports showing the composition of their workforce; however, we did not include these firms in our analysis. Accordingly, our EEO-1 analysis presented in this report may not match the EEO-1 data presented on EEOC's website. As required under the Civil Rights Act of 1964, EEOC collects periodic reports from public and private employers and unions and labor organizations that indicate the composition of their work forces by sex and by racial/ethnic category. Key among these reports is the EEO-1.

[2] EEOC defines the job category of "officials and managers" as occupations requiring administrative and managerial personnel, who set broad policies, exercise overall responsibility for execution of these policies, and direct individual departments or special phases of a firm's operation.

[3] In 2007, EEOC subdivided the "officials and managers' category into two subcategories. The first one, "Executive/Senior Level Officials and Managers," includes individuals who reside in the highest levels of organizations and plan, direct, and formulate policies, set strategy, and provide the overall direction of enterprises/organizations for the development and delivery of products or services, within the parameters approved by boards of directors or other governing bodies. The second category, "First/Mid-Level Officials and Managers," includes individuals who receive directions from Executive/Senior Level management and oversee and direct the delivery of products, services, or functions at group, regional, or divisional levels of organizations.

[4] We used monthly averages over 3 months—July, August, and September—from the Basic Monthly CPS for each year and then calculated the estimated percentages, as EEOC's EEO-1 reports are collected over this period of time every year.

[5] In our 2006 report we selected industry representatives based on a variety of criteria including whether they had received public recognition of their diversity programs or on the type of sector (such as securities or commercial banking) they were involved in. GAO-06-617.

[6] EEOC collects a variety of data on workforce diversity from federal agencies, including information pursuant to a management directive it issued in 2003 that included policy guidelines and standards for establishing and maintaining affirmative employment programs. This directive does not apply to the Federal Reserve Banks, as they are not federal agencies. EEOC MD-715 (2003).

[7] On July 21, 2010, the Consumer Financial Protection Act established CFPB as an independent bureau within the Federal Reserve System to be headed by a director. Effective July 21, 2011, CFPB assumed responsibility for certain consumer financial protection functions formerly the responsibilities of the Board of Governors of the Federal Reserve System, the Comptroller of the Currency, the Director of the Office of Thrift Supervision, FDIC, the Federal Trade Commission, NCUA, and the Secretary of the Department of Housing and Urban Development.

[8] We obtained annual EEO-1 reports from all 12 Reserve Banks, which are located in Atlanta, Boston, Chicago, Cleveland, Dallas, Kansas City, Minneapolis, New York, Philadelphia, Richmond, San Francisco, and St. Louis.

[9] These data are organized in table A3 of each MD-715 report and as part of the consolidated employer information reports for Reserve Bank EEO-1 data. For both data sets, race and ethnicity categories included Hispanic or Latino, White, Black or African American, Asian American, Native Hawaiian or Other Pacific Islander, American Indian or Alaskan Native,

and Two or More Races. Our analysis included as an Other category: Native Hawaiian or Other Pacific Islander, American Indian or Alaskan Native, and Two or More Races.

[10] We defined senior management-level as employees reported in the most senior job category by federal financial agencies and Reserve Banks. For agency MD-715 data, we considered senior management-level as officials and managers reported as "Executive/Senior Level," in each agency's A3 data tables. For Reserve Bank EEO-1 data, we considered senior management-level as "Executive/Senior Officials and Managers," reported by each Reserve Bank. Our analysis of agencywide data included all job categories reported by each agency: Executive/Senior Level, Mid-level, First-level, and Other Officials and Managers, Professionals, Technicians, Sales Workers, Administrative Support Workers, Craft Workers, Operatives, Laborers and Helpers, and Service Workers. Our analysis of bankwide data included all job categories reported by each Reserve Bank: Executive/Senior Officials and Managers, First/Mid Officials and Managers, Professionals, Technicians, Sales Workers, Administrative Support Workers, Craft Workers, Operatives, Laborers and Helpers, and Service Workers.

End Notes for Appendix II

[1] These industry sectors under the financial services industry are split according to the NAICS.

End Notes for Appendix III

[1] The agencies included FDIC, the Federal Reserve Board, NCUA, OCC, SEC, and Treasury. FHFA was established in 2008 and started reporting workforce data for 2010, and is excluded from our trend analysis. Additionally, CFPB was established in July 2011 and trend data were not available.

In: Workforce Diversity in the Financial Sector   ISBN: 978-1-62808-442-9
Editors: E. Cruz and D. Houghton   © 2013 Nova Science Publishers, Inc.

Chapter 2

FINANCIAL SERVICES INDUSTRY: OVERALL TRENDS IN MANAGEMENT-LEVEL DIVERSITY AND DIVERSITY INITIATIVES, 1993-2008. STATEMENT OF ORICE WILLIAMS BROWN, DIRECTOR, FINANCIAL MARKETS AND COMMUNITY INVESTMENT, GOVERNMENT ACCOUNTABILITY OFFICE. HEARING ON "MINORITIES AND WOMEN IN FINANCIAL REGULATORY REFORM: THE NEED FOR INCREASING PARTICIPATION AND OPPORTUNITIES FOR QUALIFIED PERSONS AND BUSINESSES"*

United States Government Accountability Office

---

* This is an edited, reformatted and augmented version of The United States Government Accountability Office publication, Presented May 10, 2010 before the House Committee on Financial Services, Subcommittees on Oversight and Investigations and Housing and Community Opportunity.

WHY GAO DID THIS STUDY

As the U.S. workforce has become increasingly diverse, many private and public sector organizations have recognized the importance of recruiting and retaining minority and women candidates for key positions. However, previous congressional hearings have raised concerns about a lack of diversity at the management level in the financial services industry, which provides services that are essential to the continued growth and economic recovery of the country. The recent financial crisis has renewed concerns about the financial services industry's commitment to workforce diversity.

This testimony discusses findings from a June 2006 GAO report (GAO-06-617), February 2008 testimony (GAO-08-445T), and more recent work on diversity in the financial services industry. Specifically, GAO assesses (1) what the available data show about diversity at the management level from 1993 through 2008 and (2) steps that the industry has taken to promote workforce diversity and the challenges involved.

To address the testimony's objectives, GAO analyzed data from the Equal Employment Opportunity Commission (EEOC); reviewed select studies; and interviewed officials from financial services firms, trade organizations, and organizations that represent minority and women professionals. To the extent possible, key statistics have been updated.

WHAT GAO FOUND

EEOC data indicate that overall diversity at the management level in the financial services industry did not change substantially from 1993 through 2008, and diversity in senior positions remains limited. In general, EEOC data show that management-level representation by minority women and men increased from 11.1 percent to 17.4 percent during that period. However, these EEOC data overstated minority representation at senior management levels, because the category includes mid-level management positions, such as assistant branch manager, that may have greater minority representation. In 2008, EEOC reported revised data for senior-level positions only, which showed that minorities held 10 percent of such positions compared with 17.4 percent of all management positions. The revised data also indicate that white males held 64 percent of senior positions in 2008, African-Americans held 2.8 percent, Hispanics 3 percent, and Asians 3.5 percent (see figure).

Financial services firms and trade groups have initiated programs to increase workforce diversity, but these initiatives face challenges. The programs include developing scholarships and internships, partnering with groups that represent minority professionals, and linking managers' compensation with their performance in promoting a diverse workforce. Some firms have developed indicators to measure progress in achieving workforce diversity. Industry officials said that among the challenges these initiatives faced were recruiting and retaining minority candidates, and gaining the "buy-in" of key employees such as the middle managers who are often responsible for implementing such programs. Without a sustained commitment to overcoming these challenges, diversity at the management level may continue to remain generally unchanged over time.

EEOC Data for Executive/Senior Level Officers and Managers in the Financial Services Industry, 2008

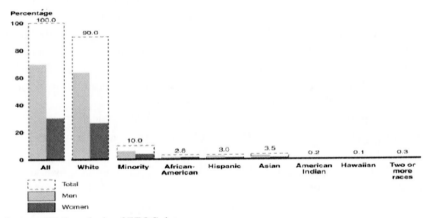

Source: GAO analysis of EEOC data.
Note: Percentages may not always add to 100 due to rounding.

Chairman Moore, Chairwoman Waters, Ranking Members Biggert and Capito, and Members of the Subcommittees:

I appreciate the opportunity to be here today to revisit our June 2006 report and subsequent 2008 testimony on diversity in the management level in the financial services industry and to discuss more recent information that we have gathered on this important topic.[1] As you know, the U.S. workforce has become increasingly diverse over the last several decades. As the composition of the workforce has changed, many private and public sector organizations have recognized the importance of recruiting and retaining minority and women candidates for key positions. In a 2005 report on diversity management, we stated that workforce diversity could benefit organizations in a variety of ways—for example, by allowing them to better meet the needs of a diverse customer base, reduce the costs associated with employee turnover, and increase staff morale.[2] However, some in the diversity management arena have raised concerns about the impact of the recent financial crisis on diversity initiatives in the financial services industry, which provides key services necessary to help restore growth and economic prosperity to the country. In hearings held by the Oversight and Investigations Subcommittee in 2004, 2006, and 2008, some witnesses stated that financial services firms—banks and securities firms, for example—had not made sufficient progress in recruiting and retaining minorities and women at the management level.[3]

My testimony summarizes the key findings from our past work, which has sought to collect, analyze, and report data and information that provide insights into diversity in the financial services industry, and to provide updated data where available. Specifically, I will discuss (1) what the available data show about diversity at the management level in the financial services industry from 1993 through 2008, and (2) the types of initiatives that the financial services industry and related organizations have taken to promote workforce diversity and the challenges involved in these efforts.

To prepare our June 2006 report, we used the Equal Employment Opportunity Commission's (EEOC) Employer Information Report (EEO-1) data on financial services firms with 100 or more employees for the period from 1993 through 2004.[4] The EEO-1 data provide information on racial/gender representation for various occupations, including "officials and managers," for a broad range of industries, including financial services. In updating our work in preparation for this testimony, we collected and analyzed EEO-1 data for financial services firms with 100 or more employees for 2005 through 2008. However, because EEOC began using an updated system for classifying industries, we cannot combine the two data sets to conduct a direct and continuous trend analysis of changes in the representation of minorities and women at the management level.[5] Nevertheless, the 2005 through 2008 EEO-1 representation data for the financial services industry can generally be compared with the EEO-1 data for 2004 and prior years. For this testimony, we also used more complete EEO-1 data that EEOC began to collect in 2007 for senior management positions.[6] EEOC, as described in this testimony, began to report data specifically for senior management positions rather than combining the data with data for mid-level management positions as had been the reporting practice prior to 2008. Our past work also involved reviewing reports on the state of workforce diversity and initiatives to increase the representation of minority and women in financial services firms and interviewing academics and officials from a variety of financial services firms and trade and professional groups.

We performed these performance audits during the periods previously described and updated this work in May 2010, in accordance with generally accepted government auditing standards. Those standards require that we plan and perform the audit to obtain sufficient, appropriate evidence to provide a reasonable basis for our findings and conclusions based on our audit objectives. We believe that the evidence obtained provides a reasonable basis for our findings and conclusions based on our audit objectives.

SUMMARY

EEO-1 data indicate that from 1993 through 2008 overall workforce diversity in management positions within the financial services industry did not change substantially, and revised EEO-1 data that EEOC began to report in 2008 indicates that diversity in senior management positions is limited. As described in our June 2006 report, EEO-1 data show that management-level representation by minority women and men increased from 11.1 percent to 15.5 percent from 1993 through 2004. The revised EEO-1 data for the period 2005 through 2008 indicate that overall minority representation at the management level increased from 15.5 to 17.4 percent. This increase was largely driven by growth in Asian representation in management positions. Asian representation increased by nearly a full percentage point, from 4.7 percent to 5.5 percent over the period, while African-American and Hispanic representation remained stable at around 6.3 percent and nearly 5 percent, respectively. While the EEO-1 data shows some increase in overall diversity in management levels from 1993 through 2008, in 2008 EEOC also began to report revised EEO-1 data for a new category specifically focused on senior-level executives and managers. The revised data indicate that the earlier data overstated the representation of women and minorities among senior executives. Specifically, the revised data indicate that minorities accounted for about 10 percent of all senior management positions in the financial services industry in 2008 while the broader measure was 17.4 percent. The revised data also indicate that white men held about 64 percent of senior management positions in 2008 while African-Americans held 2.8 percent, Hispanics 3.0 percent, and Asians 3.5 percent.

Although financial services firms and trade groups had initiated programs to increase workforce diversity, these initiatives faced challenges that may help explain why overall diversity at the management level has not changed substantially. Officials at financial services firms said that diversity was an important goal and that top leadership was committed to recruiting and retaining minority and women candidates. Some financial services firms had established scholarship and internship programs or partnered with groups that represent minority professionals. Officials from a few firms told us that they had begun linking managers' compensation and performance in promoting workforce diversity, and some firms had developed indicators (e.g., representation by minorities and women in key positions) to measure progress in achieving workforce diversity. Industry officials said that among the challenges these initiatives faced were recruiting and retaining minority candidates, as well as gaining the "buy-in" of key employees, such as the middle managers who were often responsible for implementing such programs. Without a sustained commitment to overcoming these challenges, diversity at the management level in the financial services industry may continue to remain generally unchanged over time.

BACKGROUND

We defined the financial services industry to include the following sectors:

- depository credit institutions, which include commercial banks, thrifts (savings and loan associations and savings banks), and credit unions;
- holdings and trusts, which include investment trusts, investment companies, and holding companies;
- nondepository credit institutions, which extend credit in the form of loans and include federally sponsored credit agencies, personal credit institutions, and mortgage bankers and brokers;
- the securities sector, which is made up of a variety of firms and organizations (e.g., broker-dealers) that bring together buyers and sellers of securities and commodities, manage investments, and offer financial advice; and

- the insurance sector, including carriers and insurance agents that provide protection against financial risks to policyholders in exchange for the payment of premiums.

The financial services industry is a major source of employment in the United States. EEO-1 data showed that financial services firms we reviewed for this work, which have 100 or more staff, employed over 3 million people in 2008. Moreover, according to the U.S. Bureau of Labor Statistics, employment in the financial services industry was expected to grow by 5 percent from 2008 to 2018.[7] Employment in the credit intermediation and related activities industry, which includes banks, is expected to account for 42 percent of all new jobs within the finance and insurance sector.

DIVERSITY IN THE FINANCIAL SERVICES INDUSTRY AT THE MANAGEMENT LEVEL DID NOT CHANGE SUBSTANTIALLY FROM 1993 THROUGH 2008, AND DIVERSITY IN SENIOR MANAGEMENT POSITIONS IS LIMITED

As discussed in our 2006 report, overall diversity in management-level positions did not change substantially from 1993 through 2004. Specifically, figure 1 shows that diversity in senior positions increased from 11.1 percent to 15.5 percent during that period. Regarding the change within specific groups, African-Americans increased their representation from 5.6 percent to 6.6 percent, Asians from 2.5 percent to 4.5 percent, Hispanics from 2.8 percent to 4.0 percent, and American Indians from 0.2 to 0.3 percent. Management-level representation by white women was largely unchanged at slightly more than one-third during the period, while representation by white men declined from 52.2 percent to 47.2 percent.

Revised EEO-1 data for the period 2005 through 2008 show an increase in minority representation in management positions from 15.5 percent to 17.4 percent (fig. 2).

This increase was largely driven by the growing representation of Asians in management positions—an increase of nearly a full percentage point from 4.7 percent to 5.5 percent during the period.

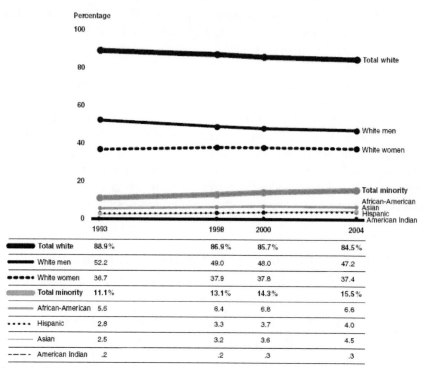

	1993	1998	2000	2004
Total white	88.9%	86.9%	85.7%	84.5%
White men	52.2	49.0	48.0	47.2
White women	36.7	37.9	37.8	37.4
Total minority	11.1%	13.1%	14.3%	15.5%
African-American	5.6	6.4	6.8	6.6
Hispanic	2.8	3.3	3.7	4.0
Asian	2.5	3.2	3.6	4.5
American Indian	.2	.2	.3	.3

Source: GAO analysis of EEOC data.
Note: Percentages may not always add to 100 due to rounding.

Figure 1. EEO-1 Data on Trends in Diversity in the Financial Services Industry at the Management Level (1993, 1998, 2000, and 2004).

Meanwhile, African-American representation remained stable at about 6.3 percent from 2005 through 2008, while Hispanic representation increased by half of a percentage point from 4.3 to 4.8 percent. Management-level representation by white women and white men both decreased by about one percentage point from 2005 through 2008.

However, before 2008 EEO-1 data generally overstated representation levels for minorities and white women in the most senior-level positions, such as chief executive officers of large investment firms or commercial banks, because the category that captured these positions—"officials and managers"—covered all management positions.

Thus, this category included lower-level positions (e.g., assistant manager of a small bank branch) that may have a higher representation of minorities and women.

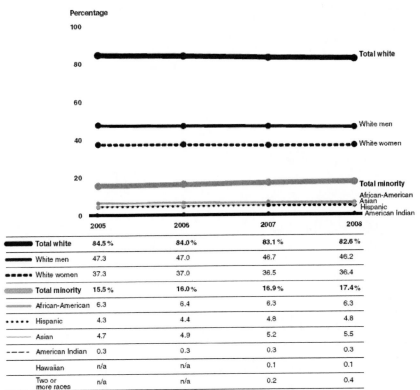

		2005	2006	2007	2008
	Total white	84.5%	84.0%	83.1%	82.6%
	White men	47.3	47.0	46.7	46.2
	White women	37.3	37.0	36.5	36.4
	Total minority	15.5%	16.0%	16.9%	17.4%
	African-American	6.3	6.4	6.3	6.3
	Hispanic	4.3	4.4	4.8	4.8
	Asian	4.7	4.9	5.2	5.5
	American Indian	0.3	0.3	0.3	0.3
	Hawaiian	n/a	n/a	0.1	0.1
	Two or more races	n/a	n/a	0.2	0.4

Source: GAO analysis of EEOC data.
Note: Percentages may not always add to 100 due to rounding.

Figure 2. EEO-1 Data on Trends in Diversity in the Financial Services Industry at the Management Level, 2005 through 2008.

Recognizing this limitation, starting in 2007 EEOC revised its data collection form for employers to divide the "officials and managers" category into two subcategories: "executive/senior-level officers and managers" and "first/midlevel officials."

EEOC's revised data, as reported in 2008, indicate that minorities accounted for 10 percent of senior positions in the financial services industry. As I discussed previously, the percentage in the broader data category was 17.4 percent. Moreover, as shown in figure 3, white men accounted for approximately 64 percent of senior-level management positions. In contrast, African Americans held 2.8 percent of such senior management positions, while Hispanics held 3.0 percent and Asians 3.5 percent.

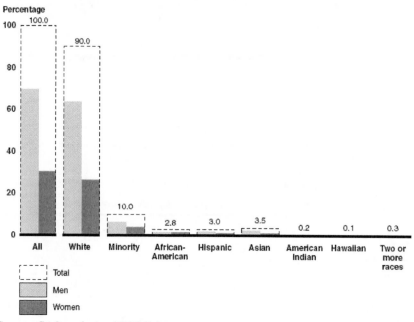

Source: GAO analysis of EEOC data.
Note: Percentages may not always add to 100 due to rounding.

Figure 3. EEO-1 Data for Executive/Senior Level Officers and Managers in the Financial Services Industry, 2008.

INITIATIVES TO PROMOTE WORKFORCE DIVERSITY IN THE FINANCIAL SERVICES INDUSTRY FACE CHALLENGES

Officials from the firms that we contacted for our previous work said that their top leadership was committed to implementing workforce diversity initiatives but noted that making such initiatives work was challenging. In particular, the officials cited ongoing difficulties in recruiting and retaining minority candidates and in gaining employees' "buy-in" for diversity initiatives, especially at the middle management level. Some firms noted that they had stepped up efforts to help ensure a diverse workforce. However, the recent financial crisis has raised questions about their ongoing commitment to initiatives and programs that are designed to promote workforce diversity.

Financial Services Firms Implemented a Variety of Diversity Initiatives

Minorities' rapid growth as a percentage of the overall U.S. population, as well as increased global competition, convinced some financial services firms that workforce diversity was a critical business strategy. Since the mid-1990s, some financial services firms have implemented a variety of initiatives designed to recruit and retain minority and women candidates to fill key positions. Officials from several banks said that they had developed scholarship and internship programs to encourage minority students to consider careers in banking. Some firms and trade organizations had also developed partnerships with groups that represent minority professionals and with local communities to recruit candidates through events such as conferences and career fairs. To help retain minorities and women, firms have established employee networks, mentoring programs, diversity training, and leadership and career development programs.

Industry studies have noted, and officials from some financial services firms we contacted confirmed, that senior managers were involved in diversity initiatives. Some of these officials also said that this level of involvement was critical to success of a program. For example, according to an official from an investment bank, the head of the firm meets with all minority and female senior executives to discuss their career development. Officials from a few commercial banks said that the banks had established diversity "councils" of senior leaders to set the vision, strategy, and direction of diversity initiatives. A 2007 industry trade group study and some officials also noted that some companies were linking managers' compensation to their progress in hiring, promoting, and retaining minority and women employees.[8] However, the study found that most companies reported that they still did not offer managers financial rewards for improving diversity performance.

This study also found that firms, overall, have significantly increased accountability for driving diversity results. For example, more firms reported that they were holding managers accountable for improving diversity. Performance reviews and management-by-objectives were the top two methods for measuring managers' diversity performance. Finally, firms whose representation of women and minorities was above the median for the survey group were considerably more likely to use certain diversity management strategies and practices.

A few firms had also developed performance indicators to measure progress in achieving diversity goals. These indicators include workforce representation, turnover, promotion of minority and women employees, and employee satisfaction survey responses. Officials from several financial services firms stated that measuring the results of diversity efforts over time was critical to the credibility of the initiatives and to justifying the investment in the resources such initiatives demanded.

Several Challenges May Have Affected the Success of Workforce Diversity Initiatives in the Financial Services Industry

While financial services firms and trade groups we contacted had launched diversity initiatives, officials from these organizations and other information suggested that several challenges may have limited the success of their efforts. These challenges include the following:

- *Recruiting minority and women candidates for management development programs.* Available data on minority students enrolled in Master of Business Administration (MBA) programs suggest that the pool of minorities, a source that may feed the "pipeline" for management-level positions within the financial services industry and other industries is a limiting factor.[9] In 2000, minorities accounted for 19 percent of all students enrolled in MBA programs in accredited U.S. schools; in 2006, that student population had risen to 25 percent. Financial services firms compete for minorities in this pool not only with one another but also with firms from other industries.
- *Fully leveraging the "internal" pipeline of minority and women employees for management-level positions.* As shown in figure 4, there are job categories within the financial services industry that generally have more overall workforce diversity than the "Executive/Senior Level Officials & Managers" category, particularly among minorities. For example, minorities held almost 25 percent of "professional" positions in the industry in 2008, compared with 10 percent of "executive/senior level officials & managers" positions. According to a 2006 EEOC report, the professional category represented a possible pipeline of available management-level candidates.[10] The EEOC report stated that the chances of minorities and women (white and minority combined) advancing from the professional category into management-level positions were lower than they were for white males.

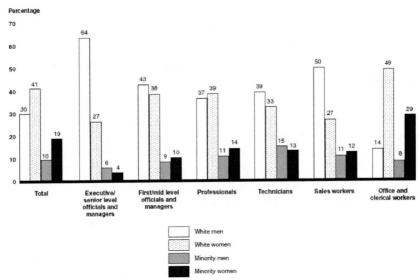

Source: GAO analysis of EEOC data.
Note: Percentages may not always add to 100 due to rounding.

Figure 4. EEO-1 Data (Percentage) on Workforce Diversity in the Financial Services Industry by Position, Gender, and Racial/Ethic Group (2008).

- Retaining minority and women candidates that are hired for key management positions. Many industry officials said that financial services firms lack a critical mass of minority men and women, particularly in senior-level positions, to serve as role models. Without a critical mass, the officials said that minority or women employees might lack the personal connections and access to informal networks that are often necessary to navigate an organization's culture and advance their careers. For example, an official from a commercial bank we contacted said he learned from staff interviews that African-Americans believed that they were not considered for promotion as often as others partly because they were excluded from informal employee networks needed for promotion or to promote advancement.
- Achieving the "buy-in" of key employees, such as middle managers. Middle managers are particularly important to the success of diversity initiatives because they are often responsible for implementing key aspects of such initiatives and for explaining them to other employees. However, some financial services industry officials said that middle managers may be focused on other aspects of their responsibilities,

such as meeting financial performance targets, rather than the importance of implementing the organization's diversity initiatives. Additionally, the officials said that implementing diversity initiatives represented a considerable cultural and organizational change for many middle managers and employees at all levels. An official from an investment bank told us that the bank had been reaching out to middle managers who oversaw minority and women employees by, for example, instituting an "inclusive manager program."

- In closing, with the implementation of a variety of diversity initiatives over the past 15 years, diversity at the management level in the financial services industry has improved but not changed substantially. Further, EEOC's new EEO-1 data provide a clearer view of diversity within senior executive ranks, showing that diversity is lower than the overall industry management diversity statistics had indicated. Initiatives to promote management diversity at all levels within financial services firms face several key challenges, such as recruiting and retaining candidates and achieving the "buy-in" of middle managers. The impact of the recent financial crisis on diversity also warrants ongoing scrutiny. Without a sustained commitment to overcoming these challenges, management diversity in the financial services industry may continue to remain largely unchanged over time.

Mr. Chairman and Madam Chairwoman, this concludes my prepared statement. I would be pleased to respond to any questions you or other members of the subcommittees may have.

End Notes

[1] GAO, Financial Services Industry: Overall Trends in Management-Level Diversity and Diversity Initiatives, 1993-2004, GAO-06-617 (Washington, D.C.: June 1, 2006) and Financial Services Industry: Overall Trends in Management-Level Diversity and Diversity Initiatives, 1993-2006, GAO-08-445T (Washington, D.C.: Feb. 7, 2008). For purposes of this testimony, we focused on changes in management-level representation over time by gender and racial/ethnic minority groups, including African-Americans, Asians, Hispanics, and American Indians.

[2] GAO, Diversity Management: Expert-Identified Leading Practices and Agency Examples, GAO-05-90 (Washington, D.C.: Jan. 14, 2005).

[3] Diversity in the Financial Services Sector; Hearing before the Comm. on Financial Services, Subcomm. on Oversight and Investigations, 110th Cong., 2nd session, (2008); Diversity:

The GAO Perspective: Hearing before the Subcomm. on Oversight and Investigations of the House Comm. on Financial Services, 109th Cong., 2nd session, (2006); and Diversity in the Financial Services Industry and Access to Capital for Minority Owned Businesses: Challenges and Opportunities; Hearing before the Comm. on Financial Services, Subcomm. on Oversight and Investigations, 108th Cong., 2nd Session (2004).

[4] For the June 2006 report, we used the EEO-1 "officials and managers" job category as the basis for our discussion of management-level diversity within the financial services industry. EEOC defines the job category of "officials and managers" as occupations requiring administrative and managerial personnel who set broad policies, exercise overall responsibility for execution of these policies, and direct individual departments or special phases of a firm's operation.

[5] Our June 2006 report describes our approach to reporting the 1993 through 2004 EEO-1 data, which used the Standard Industry Classification System (SIC). In preparing for the 2008 testimony, EEOC said that the previous approach would not be reliable for the 2006 EEO-1 data because the SIC had become increasingly unreliable over time and had been replaced by the North American Industrial Classification System.

[6] Beginning in 2007, EEOC divided the "officials and managers' category into two subcategories. The first one, "Executive/Senior Level Officials and Managers," includes individuals who reside in the highest levels of organizations and plan, direct and formulate policies, set strategy, and provide the overall direction of enterprises/organizations for the development and delivery of products or services, within the parameters approved by boards of directors or other governing bodies. The second category, "First/Mid-Level Officials and Managers," includes individuals who receive directions from Executive/Senior Level management, and oversee and direct the delivery of products, services, or functions at group, regional or divisional levels of organizations.

[7] Bureau of Labor Statistics, Occupational Outlook Handbook, 2010-11 Edition, (Washington, D.C.: December 17, 2009).

[8] See Securities Industry and Financial Markets Association, 2007 Report on U.S. Workforce Diversity and Organizational Practices (November 2007). According to SIFMA, 31 firms submitted responses, capturing demographic information on a representative sample of the industry workforce (over 330,000 employees).

[9] Association to Advance Collegiate Schools of Business, the world's largest accreditation association for business schools, conducts an annual survey called "Business School Questionnaire" of all its accredited schools. Participation in this survey is voluntary. For the year 2006, 94.3 percent of the accredited schools responded to the survey.

[10] Equal Employment Opportunity Commission, Diversity in the Finance Industry (Washington, D.C.: April 2006).

In: Workforce Diversity in the Financial Sector   ISBN: 978-1-62808-442-9
Editors: E. Cruz and D. Houghton   © 2013 Nova Science Publishers, Inc.

Chapter 3

FINANCIAL SERVICES INDUSTRY: OVERALL TRENDS IN MANAGEMENT-LEVEL DIVERSITY AND DIVERSITY INITIATIVES, 1993-2004*

United States Government Accountability Office

WHY GAO DID THIS STUDY

During a hearing in 2004 on the financial services industry, congressional members and witnesses expressed concern about the industry's lack of workforce diversity, particularly in key management-level positions. Witnesses stated that financial services firms (e.g., banks and securities firms) had not made sufficient progress in recruiting and promoting minority and women candidates for management-level positions. Concerns were also raised about the ability of minority-owned businesses to raise capital (i.e., debt or equity capital).

GAO was asked to provide an overview on the status of diversity in the financial services industry. This report discusses (1) what available data show regarding diversity at the management level in the financial services industry from 1993 through 2004, (2) the types of initiatives that financial firms and

---

* This is an edited, reformatted and augmented version of United States Government Accountability Office, Publication No. GAO-06-617, dated June 2006.

related organizations have taken to promote workforce diversity and the challenges involved, and (3) the ability of minority- and women-owned businesses to obtain access to capital in financial markets and initiatives financial institutions have taken to make capital available to these businesses.

GAO makes no recommendations in this report.

WHAT GAO FOUND

Between 1993 through 2004, overall diversity at the management level in the financial services industry did not change substantially, but increases in representation varied by racial/ethnic minority group. During that period, Equal Employment Opportunity Commission (EEOC) data show that management-level representation by minority men and women increased from 11.1 percent to 15.5 percent (see figure below). Specifically, African-Americans increased their representation from 5.6 percent to 6.6 percent, Asians from 2.5 percent to 4.5 percent, Hispanics from 2.8 percent to 4.0 percent, and American Indians from 0.2 percent to 0.3 percent. The EEOC data also show that representation by white women remained constant at slightly more than one-third whereas representation by white men declined from 52.2 percent to 47.2 percent.

Financial services firms and trade groups GAO contacted stated that they have initiated programs to increase workforce diversity, including in management-level positions, but these initiatives face challenges. The programs include developing scholarships and internships, establishing programs to foster employee retention and development, and linking managers' compensation with their performance in promoting a diverse workforce. However, firm officials said that they still face challenges in recruiting and retaining minority candidates. Some officials also said that gaining employees' "buy-in" to diversity programs was a challenge, particularly among middle managers who were often responsible for implementing key aspects of such programs.

Research reports suggest that minority- and women-owned businesses have generally faced difficulties in obtaining access to capital for several reasons such as these businesses may be concentrated in service industries and lack assets to pledge as collateral. Other studies suggest that lenders may discriminate in providing credit, but assessing lending discrimination may be complicated by limited data availability. However, some financial institutions, primarily commercial banks, said that they have developed strategies to serve minority- and women-owned businesses. These strategies include marketing existing financial products specifically to minority and women business owners.

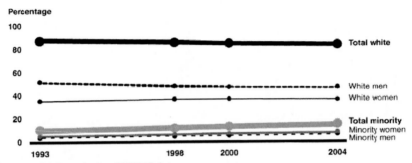

Source: GAO analysis of EEOC data.

Workforce Representation in the Financial Services Industry at the Management Level (1993, 1998, 2000, and 2004).

ABBREVIATIONS

AACSB	Association to Advance Collegiate Schools of Business
ABA	American Bankers Association
ACS	American Community Survey
AICPA	American Institute of Certified Public Accountants
CPA	certified public accountant
ECOA	Equal Credit Opportunity Act
EEO-1 data	Employer Information Report data
EEOC	Equal Employment Opportunity Commission
GMAC®	Graduate Management Admission Council®
HMDA	Home Mortgage Disclosure Act
IIABA	Independent Insurance Agents and Brokers of America
MBA	Masters of Business Administration
NAICS	North American Industry Classification System
PUMS	Public Use Microdata Sample
SBA	Small Business Administration
SBO	Survey of Business Owners
SIA	Securities Industry Association
SIC	Standard Industrial Classification

June 1, 2006

The Honorable Michael G. Oxley
Chairman

The Honorable Barney Frank
Ranking Minority Member
Committee on Financial Services
House of Representatives

The Honorable Sue W. Kelly
Chairwoman

The Honorable Luis V. Gutierrez
Ranking Minority Member
Subcommittee on Oversight and Investigations
Committee on Financial Services
House of Representatives

The Honorable David Scott
House of Representatives

At a July 2004 hearing before the Subcommittee on Oversight and Investigations of the House Committee on Financial Services, some members and witnesses expressed concern about the financial services industry's lack of workforce diversity, particularly in key management-level positions.[1] Witnesses stated that financial services firms (e.g., banks and securities firms) had not made sufficient progress in recruiting minority and women candidates for management-level positions. Concerns were also raised about the ability of minority-owned businesses to raise debt and equity capital.

This report follows up on the issues raised in the subcommittee hearing and responds to your February 2005 request that we provide an overview on the status of diversity in the financial services industry. Specifically, our objectives were to discuss (1) what the available data show regarding diversity at the management level in the financial services industry from 1993 through 2004, (2) the types of initiatives that the financial services industry and related organizations have taken to promote workforce diversity and the challenges involved, and (3) the ability of minority- and women-owned businesses to obtain access to capital in financial markets and initiatives financial institutions have taken to make capital available to these businesses. You also asked that we include information about the accounting industry, which we address separately in this report. In an earlier report, we defined workforce diversity as ways in which people in a workforce are similar and different from one another including background, education, and language skills.[2] For the purposes of this report, we focused the diversity discussion on changes in management-level representation over time by racial/ethnic minority groups (for both women and men), including African-Americans, Asian/Pacific Islanders (Asians), Hispanics or Latinos (Hispanics), and American Indians/Alaskan Natives (American Indians). We also discussed changes in management-level representation by whites (both women and men) over time. Finally, we defined raising capital as debt or equity capital obtained in conventional financial markets, such as from commercial banks or venture capital funds.

To address objective one, we primarily analyzed the Equal Employment Opportunity Commission's (EEOC) Employer Information Report (EEO-1) data for the financial services industry for employers with 100 or more employees for the years 1993, 1998, 2000, and 2004.[3] The EEO-1 data provide information on racial/ethnic and gender representation for various occupations within a broad range of industries, including financial services. We used the EEO-1 "officials and managers" job category as the basis for our discussion of management-level diversity within the financial services industry, as well as for its various sectors, such as banking and securities firms. EEOC defines the job category of "officials and managers" as occupations requiring administrative and managerial personnel, who set broad policies, exercise overall responsibility for execution of these policies, and direct individual departments or special phases of a firm's operation. First-line supervisors who engage in the same activities as the employees they supervise are reported in the same job category as the employees they supervise rather than in the "officials and managers" category. To address objectives two and three, we collected publicly available information and interviewed officials from a variety of financial services firms, including commercial banks, securities firms, and private equity/venture capital organizations. We also interviewed representatives from industry trade organizations, such as the American Bankers Association (ABA); the Securities Industry Association (SIA); Mortgage Bankers Association (Association); and the Independent Insurance Agents and Brokers of America (IIABA); federal agencies, including EEOC; the U.S. Department of Commerce's Minority Business Development Administration (MBDA); the Small Business Administration (SBA); and federal bank regulators; academics; and organizations that represent minority- and women-owned businesses, such as the U.S. Hispanic Chamber of Commerce and the National Association of Women Business Owners. We also reviewed available government and industry studies that address workforce diversity in the financial services industry and the ability of minority- and women-owned businesses to obtain access to capital.

We conducted our work from July 2005 to May 2006 in Washington, D.C., and New York City in accordance with generally accepted government auditing standards. Appendix I describes the objectives, scope, and methodology of our review in more detail. At your request, appendix II discusses overall statistics on workforce diversity in the financial services industry, and appendix III discusses workforce diversity in the accounting industry.

RESULTS IN BRIEF

From 1993 through 2004, overall diversity at the management level in the financial services industry did not change substantially, but some racial/ethnic minority groups experienced more change in representation than others. During that period, EEO-1 data show that management-level representation by minority women and men overall increased from 11.1 percent of all industry management-level positions to 15.5 percent. Specifically, African-Americans increased their management-level representation from 5.6 percent to 6.6 percent, Asians from 2.5 percent to 4.5 percent, Hispanics from 2.8 percent to 4.0 percent, and American Indians from 0.2 percent to 0.3 percent. Representation by white women remained constant at slightly more than one-third whereas representation by white men declined from 52.2 percent to 47.2 percent (overall white management-level representation declined from 88.9 percent in 1993 to 84.5 percent in 2004). Additionally, the EEO-1 data indicate that, within the financial services industry, certain sectors have a somewhat more diverse management-level workforce than others. For example, the EEO-1 data show that depository institutions, such as commercial banks, and insurance companies generally have a higher degree of representation by minorities or white women at the management level than securities firms.

Although financial services firms and trade groups have initiated programs to increase workforce diversity, including in management-level positions, these initiatives face challenges that may help explain why overall diversity at the management level did not change substantially from 1993 through 2004. According to officials from financial services firms we spoke with, diversity is an important goal, and their companies' top leadership is committed to implementing programs to recruit and retain minority and women candidates. For example, to develop a pool of minority candidates, financial services firms have established scholarship and internship programs or partnered with groups that represent minority professionals, such as the National Black Master of Business Administration Association. Additionally, officials from a few firms told us that in the last few years they have been linking managers' compensation with their performance in promoting workforce diversity. Moreover, some firms have developed performance indicators (e.g., representation by minorities and women in key positions) to measure their progress in achieving workforce diversity. However, financial services firm officials said that they still face challenges in recruiting and retaining minority candidates. Some firm officials also said that gaining employees' "buy-in" to diversity programs was a challenge, particularly among middle managers who were often responsible for implementing key aspects of such programs.

Research reports and our discussions with financial services firms and relevant trade groups suggest that minority- and women-owned businesses generally have difficulty obtaining access to capital in conventional financial markets for several reasons. A 2004 report by the MBDA stated that minority-owned businesses may have difficulty in obtaining capital because they are often concentrated in service industries and lack sufficient assets to pledge as collateral to obtain financing or because many such businesses lack an established record of creditworthiness.[4] Other studies suggest that lenders may discriminate in deciding whether to make loans to minority-owned businesses. However, assessing lending discrimination against minority- and women-owned businesses may be complicated by limited data availability. In particular, the Federal Reserve's Regulation B, which implements the Equal Credit Opportunity Act, prohibits financial institutions from requiring information on race and gender from applicants for nonmortage credit products.[5] Federal financial regulators and others have stated that Regulation B limits their capacity to monitor potential business lending discrimination. While minority- and women-owned businesses may have faced difficulties in obtaining capital from conventional sources over the years, some financial institutions, primarily commercial banks, said that they have developed strategies to serve minority- and women-owned businesses. These strategies include marketing financial products specifically to minority- and women-owned businesses, although it does not appear that these financial institutions actually changed their general underwriting standards for such businesses. In addition, some financial institutions have established programs to provide technical assistance (e.g., assistance in developing business plans) to minority-owned and women-owned businesses so that these firms are better positioned to obtain capital from conventional sources.

This report does not contain recommendations. We requested comments on a draft of this report from the Chair, U.S. Equal Employment Opportunity Commission (EEOC). EEOC provided technical comments, which we incorporated as appropriate. We also obtained comments from officials at selected industry trade associations, federal agencies, and organizations that examine access to capital issues on selected excerpts of a draft of this report. We have incorporated their comments as appropriate.

BACKGROUND

This section provides brief descriptions of the financial services industry and its component sectors, the changing demographic characteristics of the United States, and diversity management.

Overview of the Financial Services Industry

The financial services industry plays a key role in the U.S. economy by, among other things, providing vehicles, such as insured deposits, providing credit to individuals and businesses, and providing protection against certain financial risks. We defined the financial services industry to include the following sectors:

- depository credit institutions, which is the largest sector, include commercial banks, thrifts (savings and loan associations and savings banks), and credit unions;
- holdings and trusts, which include investment trusts, investment companies, and holding companies;
- nondepository credit institutions, which extend credit in the form of loans, but are not engaged in deposit banking, include federally sponsored credit agencies, personal credit institutions, and mortgage bankers and brokers;

- the securities industry, which is made up of a variety of firms and organizations (e.g., broker-dealers) that bring together buyers and sellers of securities and commodities, manage investments, and offer financial advice; and
- the insurance industry, including carriers and insurance agents, which provides protection against financial risks to policyholders in exchange for the payment of premiums.

Additionally, the financial services industry is a major source of employment in the United States. The financial services firms we reviewed for this study, which have 100 or more staff, employed nearly 3 million people in 2004, according to the EEO-1 data. According to the U.S. Bureau of Labor Statistics, employment growth in management and professional positions in the financial services industry was expected to grow at a rate of 1.2 percent annually through 2012.

Changing U.S. Demographic Characteristics and Definition of Diversity Management

According to the U.S. Census Bureau, the U.S. population is becoming more diverse by race and ethnicity. [6] In 2001, Census projected that the non-Hispanic, white share of the U.S. population would fall from 75.7 percent in 1990 to 52.5 percent in 2050, with a similar increase from the minority population during the same period. Census further projected that the largest increases would be in the Hispanic and Asian populations. According to the Census Bureau's *2004 American Community Survey* results, Hispanics are now the second largest racial/ethic group after whites. [7] The rapid growth of minorities in the Unites States may also influence its economic activities. For example, according to Census, the number of firms owned by minorities and women continues to grow faster than the number of other firms. In particular, a recent Census report based on data from the *2002 Economic Census* stated that, between 1997 and 2002, Hispanics in the United States opened new businesses at a rate three times faster than the national average. [8]

As we stated in a 2005 report, the composition of the U.S. workforce has become increasingly diverse, and many organizations are implementing diversity management initiatives. [9] Diversity management is a process intended to create and maintain a positive work environment that values individuals' similarities and differences, so that all can reach their potential and maximize their contributions to an organization's strategic goals and objectives. On the basis of a literature review and discussions with experts, we identified nine leading diversity management principles: (1) top leadership commitment, (2) diversity as part of an organization's strategic plan, (3) diversity linked to performance, (4) measurement, (5) accountability, (6) succession planning, (7) recruitment, (8) employee involvement, and (9) diversity training.

DIVERSITY IN THE FINANCIAL SERVICES INDUSTRY AT THE MANAGEMENT LEVEL DID NOT CHANGE SUBSTANTIALLY

EEO-1 data indicate that overall diversity among officials and managers within the financial services industry did not change substantially from 1993 through 2004, but that changes by racial/ethnic group varied. The EEO-1 data also show that certain financial sectors, such as depositories, including commercial banks, are somewhat more diverse at the management level than others, including securities firms. Additionally, EEO-1 data do not show material differences in management-level diversity based on the size of individual firms within the financial services industry.

Overview of Management-Level Diversity

Figure 1 shows the representation of minorities and whites at the management level within the financial services industry in 1993, 1998, 2000, and 2004 from EEO-1 data.[10] Management-level representation by minorities increased from 11.1 percent to 15.5 percent during the period, while representation by whites declined correspondingly from 88.9 percent to 84.5 percent. Management-level representation by white men declined from 52.2 percent to 47.2 percent during the period while the percentage of management positions held by white women was largely unchanged at slightly more than one-third.

Existing EEO-1 data may actually overstate representation levels for minorities and white women in the most senior-level positions because the "officials and managers" category includes lower- and mid-level management positions that may have higher representations of minorities and white women. According to an EEOC official we spoke with, examples for "officials and managers" would range from the Chief Executive Officer from a major investment bank to an Assistant Branch Manager of a small regional bank. A revised EEO-1 form for employers that becomes effective with the 2007 reporting year divides the category of "officials and managers" into two hierarchical sub-categories based on responsibility and influence within the organization: "executive/senior level officials and managers" and "first/mid-level officials." According to a trade association that commented on the revised EEO-1 form, collecting information about officials and managers in this manner will enable EEO-1 to more accurately report on the discriminatory artificial barriers (the "glass ceiling") that hinder the advancement of minorities and white women to more senior-level positions.

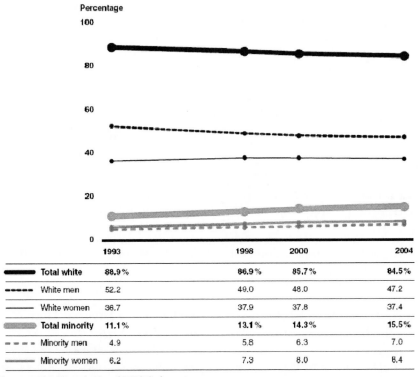

		1993	1998	2000	2004
▬	Total white	88.9%	86.9%	85.7%	84.5%
▬▬	White men	52.2	49.0	48.0	47.2
───	White women	36.7	37.9	37.8	37.4
▨	Total minority	11.1%	13.1%	14.3%	15.5%
─ ─ ─	Minority men	4.9	5.8	6.3	7.0
───	Minority women	6.2	7.3	8.0	8.4

Source: GAO analysis of EEOC data.

Note: Percentages may not always add to 100 due to rounding.

Figure 1. EEO-1 Data on Trends in Workforce Diversity in the Financial Services Industry at the Management Level (1993, 1998, 2000, and 2004).

Figure 2 provides EEO-1 data for individual minority groups and illustrates their trends in representation at the management level, which varied by group. African-American representation increased from 5.6 percent in 1993 to 6.8 percent in 2000 but declined to 6.6 percent in 2004. Representation by Hispanics and Asians also increased, with both groups representing 4 percent or more of industry officers and managers by 2004. Representation by American Indians remained well under 1 percent of all management-level positions.

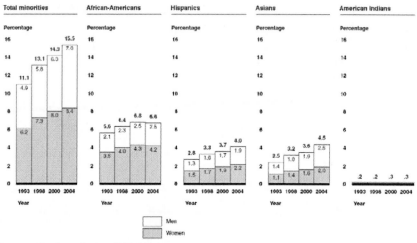

Source: GAO analysis of EEOC data.
Note: Percentages may not always add exactly due to rounding.

Figure 2. EEO-1 Data on Trends in Workforce Diversity in the Financial Services Industry at the Management Level by Racial/Ethnic Group and Gender (1993, 1998, 2000, and 2004).

Certain Financial Sectors Are Somewhat More Diverse Than Others, but Diversity Does Not Vary by Firm Size

EEO-1 data show that the depository and nondepository credit sectors, as well as the insurance sector, were somewhat more diverse in specific categories at the management level than the securities and holdings and trust sectors (see fig. 3). For example, in 2004, the percentage of management-level positions held by minorities ranged from a high of 19.9 percent for nondepository credit institutions (e.g., mortgage bankers and brokers) to a low of 12.4 percent for holdings and trusts (e.g., investment companies). The share of positions held by white women varied from a high of 40.8 percent in the insurance sector to a low of 27.4 percent among securities firms. The percentage of white men in management-level positions ranged from a high of 57.5 percent in the securities sector to a low of 44.0 percent in both the depository (e.g., commercial banks) and nondepository credit sectors. Consistent with the EEOC data, a 2005 SIA study we reviewed found limited diversity among key positions in the securities sector.[11]

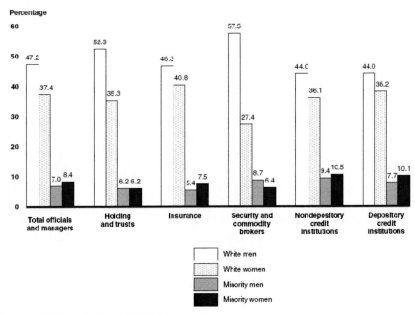

Source: GAO analysis of EEOC data.
Note: Percentages may not always add to 100 due to rounding.

Figure 3. EEO-1 Data on Workforce Diversity in the Financial Services Industry at the Management Level by Sector (2004).

EEO-1 data also show that the representation of minorities and whites at the management level in financial services firms generally does not vary by firm size (see fig. 4). Specifically, we did not find a material difference in the diversity of those in management-level positions among firms with 100 to 249 employees, 250 to 999 employees, and more than 1,000 employees.

There were some variations across financial sectors by size.[12] However, we note that SIA's 2005 study of securities firms did find variation in diversity by firm size for a variety of positions within the securities sector.[13]

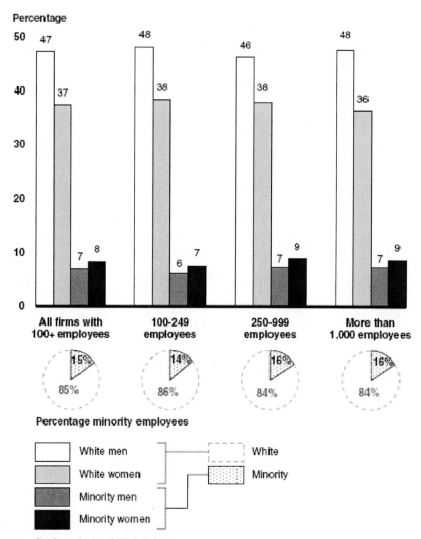

Source: GAO analysis of EEOC data.
Note: Percentages may not always add exactly due to rounding.

Figure 4. EEO-1 Data on Workforce Diversity in the Financial Services Industry at the Management Level by Firm Size (2004).

INITIATIVES TO PROMOTE WORKFORCE DIVERSITY IN THE FINANCIAL SERVICES INDUSTRY FACE CHALLENGES

Officials from financial services firms and industry trade associations we contacted stated that the rapid growth of minorities as a percentage of the overall U.S. population and increased global competition have convinced their organizations that workforce diversity is a critical business strategy. Financial firm officials we spoke with said that their top leadership was committed to implementing a variety of workforce diversity programs to help enable their organizations to take advantage of the full range of available talent to fill critical positions and to maintain their firms' competitive position. However, officials from financial services firms and trade associations also described the challenges they faced in implementing these initiatives, such as ongoing difficulties in recruiting and retaining minority candidates and in gaining commitment from employees to support diversity initiatives, especially at the middle management level.

Financial Services Firms Have Implemented a Variety of Diversity Initiatives

Over the past decade, the financial services firms we contacted have implemented a variety of initiatives to increase workforce diversity, including programs designed to recruit and retain minority and women candidates to fill key positions. Some bank officials said that they had developed scholarship and internship programs to encourage minority high school and college students to consider careers in banking with the goal of increasing the diversity of future applicant pools. Some firms have established formal relationships with colleges and Masters of Business Administration (MBA) programs to recruit minority students from these institutions. Some firms and trade organizations have also developed partnerships with groups that represent minority professionals, such as the National Black MBA Association and the National Society of Hispanic MBAs, as well as with local communities to recruit candidates, using events such as conferences and career fairs. Officials from other firms said that the goal of partnerships was to build long-term relationships with professional associations and communities and to increase the visibility of financial services firms among potential employees.

Officials from financial services firms also said that they had developed programs to foster the retention and professional growth of minority and women employees. Specifically, these firms have

- encouraged the establishment of employee networks. For example, a commercial bank official told us that, since 2003, the company had established 22 different employee networks that enabled employees from various backgrounds to meet each other, share ideas, and create informal mentoring opportunities.
- established mentoring programs. For example, an official from another commercial bank told us that the company had a Web-based program that allowed employees of all backgrounds to connect with one another and to find potential mentors.
- instituted diversity training programs. Officials from financial services firms said that these training programs increase employees' sensitivity to and awareness of workforce diversity issues and helped staff deal effectively with colleagues from different backgrounds. One commercial bank we contacted requires its managers to take a 3- to 5-day training course on dealing with a diverse workforce. The training stressed the concept of workforce diversity and provided a forum in which employees spoke about their differences through role-playing modules. The bank has also developed a diversity tool kit and certification program as part of the training.
- established leadership and career development programs. For example, an official from an investment bank told us that the head of the firm would meet with every minority and woman senior executive to discuss his or her career development. For lower-level individuals, the investment bank official said that the organization had created a career development committee to serve as a forum for discussions on career advancement.

Officials from some financial services firms we contacted as well as industry studies noted that that financial services firms' senior managers were involved in diversity initiatives. For example, SIA's 2005 study on workforce diversity in the securities industry found that almost half of the 48 securities firms surveyed had full-time senior managers dedicated to diversity initiatives. According to a report from an executive membership organization, an investment bank had developed a program that involved lower-level employees from diverse backgrounds, along with their senior managers, to develop diversity initiatives. Moreover, officials from a few commercial banks that we interviewed said that the banks had established diversity "councils" of senior leaders to set the vision, strategy, and direction of diversity initiatives. The 2005 SIA study and a few of the firm officials we spoke with also suggested that some companies have instituted programs that link managers' compensation with progress made toward promoting workforce diversity. Officials from one investment bank said that managers of each business unit reported directly to the company's Chief Executive Officer who determined their bonuses in part based on the unit's progress in hiring, promoting, and retaining minority and women employees.

According to some officials from financial services firms, their firms have also developed performance indicators to measure progress in achieving diversity goals. These indicators include workforce representation, turnover, promotion of minority and women employees, and internal employee satisfaction survey responses. An official from a commercial bank said that the company monitored the number of job openings, the number of minority and women candidates who applied for each position, the number of such candidates who interviewed for open positions, and the number hired. In addition, a few officials from financial services firms told us that they had developed additional indicators such as promotion rates for minorities and whites and compensation equity across ranks for minorities and whites. Officials from several financial services firms stated that measuring the results of diversity efforts over time was critical to the credibility of the initiatives and to justifying the investments in the resources such initiatives demanded.

Several Financial Services Trade Organizations Have Promoted Workforce Diversity

Financial services trade organizations from the securities, commercial banking, and insurance sectors that we contacted have been involved in promoting workforce diversity. The following are some examples:

- In 1996 SIA formed a "diversity committee" of senior-level executives from the securities industry to assist SIA's member firms in developing their diversity initiatives and in their efforts to market to diverse customers. This committee has begun a number of initiatives, such as developing diversity management tool kits, conducting industry demographic and diversity management research, and holding conferences. SIA's diversity tool kit provides step-by-step guidelines on establishing diversity initiatives, including identifying ways to recruit and retain diverse candidates, overcoming challenges, measuring the results of diversity initiatives, and creating strategies for transforming a firm's culture. In addition, since 1999 SIA has been conducting an industry-wide diversity survey every 2 years to help its members measure their progress toward increasing workforce diversity. The survey includes aggregated data that measure the number of minority and women employees in the securities industry at various job levels and a profile of securities industry activities designed to increase workforce diversity. In 2005, SIA held its first diversity and human resources conference, which was designed so that human resources and senior-level managers could share best practices and current strategies and trends in human resource management and diversity.

- The American Bankers Association collaborated with the Department of Labor's Office of Federal Contract Compliance Programs in 1997 to identify key issues that banks should consider in recruiting and hiring employees in order to create fair and equal employment opportunities. The issues include managing the application process and selecting candidates in a way that ensures the equal and consistent treatment of all job applications.

- The Independent Insurance Agents and Brokers of America (IIABA) established the IIABA Diversity Task Force in 2002 to promote diversity within the insurance agent community. The task force is charged with fostering a profitable independent agency force that reflects, represents, and capitalizes on the opportunities of the diverse U.S. population. Among its activities, the diversity task force is developing a database of minority insurance agents and minority-owned insurance agencies as a way to help insurance carriers seeking to expand their business with a diverse agent base and potentially reach out to urban areas and underserved markets. According to IIABA, the task force has just completed a tool kit for IIABA state associations, volunteer leadership, and staff. This step-by-step guide advises state associations on how to recruit and retain a diverse membership through their governance, products, service offerings, and association activities. In addition, IIABA participates in a program to educate high school and community college students on careers in insurance, financial services, and risk management and encourages students to pursue careers in the insurance industry.

- The Mortgage Bankers Association (Association) has established plans and programs to increase the diversity of its own leadership, as well as to promote diversity within the Association's member firms in 2005. The Association plans to increase diversity within its leadership ranks by 30 percent by September 2007 and has asked member firms to recommend potential candidates. To help member firms expand the pool of qualified diverse employees in the real estate finance industry, the Association has instituted a scholarship program called "Path to Diversity," which awards between 20 and 30 scholarships per year to minority employees and interns from member firms. Recipients can take courses at CampusMBA, the Association's training center for real estate finance, in order to further their professional growth and development in the mortgage industry.

Several Challenges May Have Affected the Success of Initiatives Designed to Increase Workforce Diversity in the Financial Services Industry

Although financial services firms and trade organizations we contacted have launched diversity initiatives, they cited a variety of challenges that may have limited their success. First, the officials said that the industry faces ongoing challenges in recruiting minority and women candidates even though firms may have established scholarship and internship programs and partnered with professional organizations. According to officials responsible for promoting workforce diversity from several firms, the industry lacks a critical mass of minority and women employees, especially at the senior levels, to serve as role models to attract other minorities to the industry. Officials from an investment bank and a commercial bank also told us that the supply (or "pipeline") of minority and women candidates in line for senior or management-level positions was limited in some geographic areas and that recruiting a diverse talent pool takes time and effort. Officials from an investment bank said that their firm typically required a high degree of specialization in finance for key positions. An official from another investment bank noted that minority candidates with these skills were very much in demand and usually receive multiple job offers.

Available data on minorities enrolled in and graduated from MBA programs provide some support for the contention that there is a limited external pool that could feed the "pipeline" for some management-level positions within the financial services industry, as well as other industries. According to the Department of Labor, many top executives from all industries, including the financial services industry, have a bachelor's degree or higher in business administration. MBA degrees are also typically required for many management development programs, according to an official from a commercial bank and an official from a foundation that provides scholarships to minority MBA students. We obtained data from the Association to Advance Collegiate Schools of Business (AACSB) on the percentage of students enrolled in MBA degree programs in accredited AACSB schools in the United States from year 2000 to 2004.[14] As shown in table 1, minorities accounted for 19 percent of all students enrolled in accredited MBA programs in 2000 and 23 percent in 2004. African-American and Hispanic enrollment in MBA programs was generally stable during that period, and both groups accounted for 6 and 5 percent of enrollment, respectively, in 2004. Asian representation increased from 9 percent in 2000 to 11 percent in 2004. Other data indicate that MBA degrees awarded may be lower than the MBA enrollment data reported by AACSB. For example, Graduate Management Admission Council[®] (GMAC[®]) data indicate that minorities in its survey sample accounted for 16 percent of MBA graduates in 2004 versus 23 percent minority enrollment during the same year as reported by AACSB.[15] Because financial services firms compete with one another, as well as with companies from other industries to recruit minority MBA graduates, their capacity to increase diversity at the management level may be limited.

Table 1. AACSB Demographic Data of Students Reported Enrolled in MBA Degree Programs at AACSB Accredited Business Schools in the United States by Racial/Ethnic Group (2000-2004)

| Year | White | Minority | | | | Total minority |
		African-American	Hispanic	Asian	American Indian	
2000	81%	5%	5%	9%	a	19%
2001	80	6	5	10	a	20
2002	80	5	5	10	a	20
2003	78	6	5	11	a	22
2004	77%	6%	5%	11%	1%	23%

Source: GAO analysis of AACSB data.

Note: Percentages may not always add exactly due to rounding. [a]Less than 1 percent.

Other evidence suggests that the financial services industry may not be fully leveraging its "internal" pipeline of minority and women employees for management-level positions. As shown in figure 5, there are job categories within the financial services industry that generally have more overall workforce diversity than the "officials and managers" category, particularly among minorities. For example, minorities held 22 percent of professional positions as compared with 15 percent of "officials and managers" positions in 2004. See appendix II for more information on the specific number of employees within other job categories, as well as more specific breakouts of various minority groups by sector.

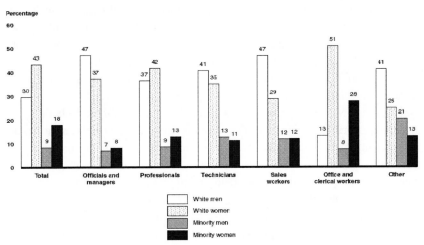

Source: GAO analysis of EEOC data.
Note: Percentages may not always add to 100 due to rounding.

Figure 5. EEO-1 Data (Percentage) on Workforce Diversity in the Financial Services Industry by Position, Racial/Ethnic Group, and Gender (2004).

According to a recent EEOC report, which used 2003 EEO-1 data, the professional category represented a likely pipeline of internal candidates for management-level positions within the industry.[16] Compared with white males, the EEOC study found that the chances of minorities and women (white and minority combined) advancing from the professional category into management-level positions were low. The study also found that the chances of Asians (women and men) advancing into management-level positions from the professional category were particularly low. Although EEOC said there are limitations to its analysis, the agency suggests that the findings could be used as a preliminary screening device designed to detect potential disparities in management-level opportunities for minorities and women.[17]

Following are descriptions of the job categories in EEO-1 data from EEOC: (1) "officials and managers": occupations requiring administrative and management personnel who set broad policies, exercise overall responsibility for execution of these policies, and direct individual departments or special phases of a firm's operations; (2) "professionals": occupations requiring either college graduation or experience of such kind and amount as to provide a comparable background; (3) "technicians": occupations requiring a combination of basic scientific knowledge and manual skill that can be obtained through 2 years of post high school education; (4) "sales workers": occupations engaging wholly or primarily in direct selling; (5) "office and clerical": includes all clerical-type work regardless of level of difficulty, where the activities are predominantly nonmanual; and (6) the category "other" includes craft workers, operatives, laborers, and service workers.

Many officials from financial services firms, industry trade groups, and associations that represent minority professionals agreed that retaining minority and women employees represented one of the biggest challenges to promoting workforce diversity. The officials said that one reason minority and women employees may leave their positions after a short period is that the industry, as described previously, lacks a critical mass of minority women and men, particularly in senior-level positions, to serve as role models. Without a critical mass, the officials said that minority or women employees may lack the personal connections and access to informal networks that are often necessary to navigate an organization's culture and advance their careers. For example, an official from a commercial bank we contacted said he learned from staff interviews that African-Americans believed that they were not considered for promotion as often as others partly because they were excluded from informal employee networks.

While firms may have instituted programs to involve managers in diversity initiatives, some industry officials said that achieving commitment, or "buy-in," can still pose challenges. Other officials said that achieving the commitment of middle managers is particularly important because these managers are often responsible for implementing key aspects of the diversity initiatives, as well as explaining them to their staffs. However, the officials said that middle managers may be focused on other aspects of their responsibilities, such as meeting financial performance targets, rather than the importance of implementing the organization's diversity initiatives. Additionally, the officials said that implementing diversity initiatives represents a considerable cultural and organizational change for many middle managers and employees at all levels. An official from an investment bank told us that the bank has been reaching out to middle managers who oversee minority and woman employees by, for example, instituting an "inclusive manager program." According to the official, the program helps managers examine subtle inequities and different managerial and working styles that may affect their relationships with minority and women employees.

MINORITY- AND WOMEN-OWNED BUSINESSES OFTEN FACE DIFFICULTIES IN OBTAINING CAPITAL, BUT SOME FINANCIAL SERVICES FIRMS HAVE DEVELOPED STRATEGIES TO ASSIST THEM

Studies and reports, as well as interviews we conducted, suggest that minority- and women-owned businesses have faced challenges obtaining capital (primarily bank credit) in conventional financial markets for several business reasons, such as the concentration of these businesses in the service sector and relative lack of a credit history.[18] Other studies suggest that lenders may discriminate, particularly against minority-owned businesses. However, assessing lending discrimination against minority-owned businesses may be complicated by limited data availability. Available research also suggests that factors, including business characteristics, introduce challenges for both minority- and women-owned businesses in obtaining access to equity capital.[19] However, some financial institutions, primarily commercial banks, have recently developed strategies to market their loan products to minority- and women-owned businesses or are offering technical assistance to them.

Research Suggests That Business Characteristics May Affect Minority- and Women-Owned Businesses' Access to Commercial Loans

Reports issued by the MBDA, SBA, and academic researchers, as well as interviews we conducted with commercial banks, minority-owned banks, and trade groups representing minority- and women-owned businesses suggest that minority- and women-owned businesses may face challenges in obtaining commercial bank credit.[20] The reports and interviews typically cite several business characteristics shared by both minority-owned firms and, in most cases, women-owned firms that may compromise their ability to obtain bank credit as follows:

- First, recent MBDA reports found that many minority-owned businesses in the United States are concentrated in retail and service industries, which have relatively low average annual capital expenditures for equipment.[21] Low capital expenditures are an attractive feature for start-up businesses, but with limited assets to pledge as collateral against loans, these businesses often have difficulty obtaining financing. According to the U.S. Census Bureau's *2002 Survey of Business Owners*, approximately 61 percent of minority-owned businesses and approximately 55 percent of women-owned firms operate in the service sectors as compared to about 52 percent of all U.S. firms.[22]

- Second, the Census Bureau's *2002 Survey of Business Owners* indicated that many minority- and women-owned businesses were start-ups or relatively new and, therefore, might not have a history of sound financial performance to present when applying for credit. Some officials from a private research organization and a trade group official we contacted said that banks are reluctant to lend to start-up businesses because of the costs involved in assessing the prospects for such businesses and in monitoring their performance over time.

- Third, the relatively small size and lack of technical experience of some minority-owned businesses may affect their ability to obtain bank credit.[23] For example, an MDBA report stated that minority businesses often need extensive mentoring and technical assistance such as help developing business plans in addition to financing.[24]

Other Studies Suggest That Discrimination May Limit Minority-Owned Businesses' Ability to Obtain Commercial Loans

Several other studies suggest that discrimination may also be a reason that minority-owned businesses face challenges obtaining commercial loans. For example, a 2005 SBA report on the small business economy summarized previous studies by researchers reporting on lending discrimination.[25] These previous studies found that minority-owned businesses had a higher probability of having their loans denied and would likely pay higher interest rates than white-owned businesses, even after controlling for differences in creditworthiness and other factors.[26] For example, a study found that given comparable loan applications—by African-American and Hispanic-owned firms and white-owned firms—the applications by the African-American and Hispanic-owned firms were more likely to be denied.[27] Another study found that minorities had higher denial rates even after controlling for personal net worth and homeownership.[28] The SBA report concludes that lending discrimination is likely to discourage would-be minority entrepreneurs and reduce the longevity of minority-owned businesses.

Another 2005 report issued by SBA also found that minority-owned businesses face some restrictions in access to credit.[29] This study investigated possible restricted access to credit for minority- and women-owned businesses by focusing on two types of credit—"relationship loans" (lines of credit) and "transaction loans" (commercial mortgages, equipment loans, and other loans) from commercial banks and nonbanks, such as finance companies.[30] The researchers found that minority business owners were more likely to have transaction loans from nonbanks and less likely to have bank loans of any kind. The researchers also found that African-American and Hispanic business owners have a greater probability of having either type of loan denied than white male owners.[31] The researchers did not find evidence suggesting that women or Asian business owners faced loan denial probabilities different from those of firms led by white, male-owned firms.

Although studies have found potential lender discrimination against minority-owned businesses, assessing such discrimination may be complicated by limited data availability. The Federal Reserve's Regulation B, which implements the Equal Credit Opportunity Act, prohibits financial institutions from requiring information on race and gender from applicants for nonmortgage credit products.[32] Although the regulation was implemented to prevent the information from being used to discriminate against underserved groups, some federal financial regulators have stated that removing the prohibition would allow them to better monitor and enforce laws prohibiting discrimination in lending. We note that under the Home Mortgage Disclosure Act (HMDA), lenders are required to collect and report data on racial and gender characteristics of applicants for mortgage loans. Researchers have used HMDA data to assess potential mortgage lending discrimination by financial institutions. In contrast, the studies we reviewed on lending discrimination against minority and small business tend to rely on surveys of small businesses by the Federal Reserve or the Census rather than on lending data obtained directly from financial institutions.

Many Minority- and Women-Owned Businesses May Also Face Difficulties Raising Equity Capital

According to available research, many minority- and women-owned businesses face challenges in raising equity capital—such as, from venture capital firms.

For example, one study estimated that only $2 billion of the $95 billion available in the private equity market in 1999 was managed by companies that focused on supplying capital to entrepreneurs from traditionally underserved markets, such as minority-owned businesses.[33] Moreover, according to a study by a private research organization, in 2003 only 4 percent of women-owned businesses with $1 million or more in revenue had been funded through private equity capital as compared with 11 percent of male-owned businesses with revenues of $1 million or more.[34]

According to studies and reports by private research organizations, some of the same types of business characteristics that may affect the ability of many minority- and women-owned businesses to obtain bank credit also limit their capacity to raise equity capital.[35] For example, industry reports and industry representatives that we contacted state that venture capitalists place a high priority on the management and technical skills companies; whereas some minority-owned businesses may lack a proven track record of such expertise.

Although venture capital firms may not have traditionally invested in minority-owned businesses, a recent study suggests that firms that do focus on such entities can earn rates of return comparable to those earned on mainstream private equity investments.[36] This study, funded by a private foundation, found that venture capital funds that specialize in investing in minority-owned businesses were relatively profitable compared with a private equity performance index.

According to the study, the venture capital funds that specialized in minority-owned businesses invested in a more diverse portfolio of businesses than the typical venture capital fund, which typically focuses on high-tech companies. The study found that investing in broad portfolios helped mitigate the losses associated with the downturn in the high-tech sector for firms that focused on minority-owned businesses.

Some Commercial Banks Have Developed Programs for Minority- and Women-Owned Businesses

While minority- and women-owned businesses may have traditionally faced challenges in obtaining capital, as noted earlier, Census data indicate that such businesses are forming rapidly. Officials from some financial institutions we contacted, primarily large commercial banks, told us that they are reaching out to minority- and women-owned businesses.

Some commercial banks are marketing their financial products to minority- and women-owned businesses by, for example, printing financial services brochures in various languages and assigning senior executives with diverse backgrounds to serve as the spokespersons for the institutions efforts to reach out to targeted groups (e.g., a bank may designate an Asian executive as the point person for Asian communities). However, officials at a bank and a trade organization told us that the loan products marketed to minority- and women-owned businesses did not differ from those marketed to other businesses and that underwriting standards had not changed.

Bank officials also said that their companies had established partnerships with trade and community organizations for minorities and women to reach out to their businesses. Partnering allows the banks to locate minority- and women-owned businesses and gather information about specific groups of business owners. Bank officials said that such partnerships had been an effective means of increasing their business with these target groups.

Finally, officials from some banks said that they educate potential business clients by providing technical assistance through financial workshops and seminars on various issues such as developing business plans and obtaining commercial bank loans. Other bank officials said that their staffs work with individual minority- or women-owned businesses to provide technical assistance.

Officials from banks with strategies to market to minority- and women-owned businesses said that they faced some challenges in implementing such programs. Many of the bank officials told us that it was time-consuming to train their staff to reach out to minority- and women-owned businesses and provide technical assistance to these potential business customers. In addition, an official from a bank said that Regulation B limited the bank's ability to measure the success of its outreach efforts. The official said that because of Regulation B the bank could only estimate the success of its efforts using estimates of the number of loans it made to minority- and women-owned businesses.

AGENCY COMMENTS AND OUR EVALUATION

We requested comments on a draft of this report from the Chair, U.S. Equal Employment Opportunity Commission (EEOC). We received technical comments from EEOC and incorporated their comments into this report as appropriate.

We also requested comments on selected excerpts of a draft of this report from 12 industry trade associations, federal agencies, and organizations that examine access to capital issues. We received technical comments from 4 of the 12 associations, agencies, and organizations and incorporated their comments into this report as appropriate. The remaining eight either informed us that they had "no comments" or did not respond to our request.

Orice M. Williams
Director,
Financial Markets and Community Investment

APPENDIX I: OBJECTIVES, SCOPE, AND METHODOLOGY

The objectives of our report were to discuss (1) what the available data show regarding diversity at the management level in the financial services industry, from 1993 through 2004; (2) the types of initiatives that the financial services industry and related organizations have taken to promote workforce diversity and the challenges involved; and (3) the ability of minority and women-owned businesses to obtain access to capital in financial markets and initiatives financial institutions have recently taken to make capital available to these businesses.

To address objective one, we requested Employer Information Reports (EEO-1) data from the Equal Employment Opportunities Commission (EEOC) for the financial services industry. The EEO-1 data, which is reported annually generally by firms with 100 or more employees, provides information on race/ethnicity and gender for various occupations, within various industries, including financial services.[1]

We used the racial/ethnic groups specified by EEOC; whites, not of Hispanic origin (whites); Asians or Pacific Islanders (Asians); Blacks, not of Hispanic origin (African-Americans); Hispanics or Latinos (Hispanics); and American Indians or Alaskan Natives (American Indians) for our analysis. The

EEO-1 occupations are officials and managers, professional, technicians, sales workers, clerical workers, and others. The other category includes laborers, craft workers, operatives, and service workers. We defined the financial services industry to include the following five sectors: depository credit institutions (including commercial banks), holdings and trusts (including investment companies), non-depository credit institutions (such as mortgage bankers), securities firms, and insurance (carriers and agents). We also requested and analyzed EEO-1 data for the accounting industry.

We chose to use the EEO-1 database because it is was designed to provide information on representation by a variety of groups within a range of occupations and industries, covered many employers, and had been collected in a standardized fashion for many years. Although the EEO-1 data generally do not capture information from small businesses with less than 100 employees, we believe, due to their annual mandatory reporting, they allow us to characterize the financial services industry of firms with 100 or more employees.

We also corroborated the EEO-1 data with other available studies, particularly a 2005 study by the Securities Industry Association on diversity within the securities sector.[2] We did consider other sources of data besides EEO-1, but chose not to use them for a variety of reasons including their being more limited or less current.[3]

We requested and analyzed the EEO-1 data, focusing on the "officials and managers" category, for the years 1993, 1998, 2000, and 2004 for financial services firms having 100 or more employees. We compared that data from the selected years to determine how the composition of management-level staff had changed since 1993. We also analyzed the data based on the number of employees in the firm or firm size. The four firm size categories we used were 100 or more employees, 100-249 employees, 250-999 employees, and 1,000 or more employees.

We also requested EEO-1 data for the accounting industry for 2004, and therefore did not perform a trend analysis. The scope of our work did not include developing appropriate benchmarks to assess the extent of workforce diversity within the financial services industry.

EEOC collects EEO-1 data from companies in a manner that allowed us to specify our data request and analysis by financial sector (e.g., commercial banking or securities). EEOC assigns each firm a code based on its primary activity (referred to as the North American Industry Classification System [NAICS] or the Standard Industrial Classification [SIC]). For example, a commercial bank will have a specific code denoting commercial banking, whereas a securities firm would have its own securities code. In addition, EEOC assigns codes to companies and their subsidiaries based on their primary line of business.

For example, a commercial bank with an insurance subsidiary would have a separate code for that subsidiary. By requesting the EEO-1 data by the relevant codes, we were able to separate the different financial services businesses within a firm and then aggregate the data by sector. Although the NAICS replaced the SIC in 1997, EEOC staff are to assign both codes to each firm that existed prior to 2002 to ensure consistency.[4]

We conducted a limited analysis to assess the reliability of the EEO-1 data. To do so, we interviewed EEOC officials regarding how the data are collected and verified as well as to identify potential data limitations. EEOC has conducted a series of data reliability analyses for EEO-1 data to verify the consistency of the data over time.

For example, EEOC reviewed the 2003 EEO-1 data for its report on diversity in the financial services industry.[5] As part of this review, EEOC deleted 81 of the 13,000 establishments because the data for the deleted establishments were not consistent year to year. The EEOC staff do not verify the EEO-1 data, which are self-reported by firms, but they do review the trends of the data submitted. For example, EEOC staff look for major fluctuations in job classifications within an industry. On the basis of this analysis, we concluded that the EEO-1 data are sufficiently reliable for our purposes.

To address objective two, we interviewed a range of financial services firms, including commercial banks and securities firms. We also interviewed representatives from a large accounting firm to discuss workforce diversity in the accounting industry.

We chose these firms for a variety of reasons including whether they have ever received public recognition of their diversity programs or on the basis of recommendations from industry officials. We also interviewed representatives from industry trade organizations such as the American Bankers Association, the Securities Industry Association, the Independent Insurance Agents and Brokers of America, the American Institute of Certified Public Accountants, and Catalyst, which is a private research firm. We reviewed the trade organizations' available studies and reports to document the state of diversity within the different sectors of the financial services industry.

In addition, we reviewed publicly available data on firms' programs by searching their Web sites. We also interviewed representatives of federal agencies such as the Bureau of Labor Statistics of the Department of Labor, the Minority Business Development Agency of the Department of Commerce, the Small Business Administration, and federal bank regulators. Additionally, we collected and analyzed demographic data on enrollment in accredited Masters of Business Administration (MBA) programs from Association to Advance Collegiate Schools of Business and MBA graduation data from the Graduate Management Admissions Council®.

To address objective three, we reviewed 20 available studies and reports from federal agencies, such as the Small Business Administration and the Minority Business Development Agency, and academic studies on the ability of minority- and women-owned businesses to access credit. We also interviewed officials from banks, investment firms and private equity/venture capital firms to discuss their initiatives to provide capital to minority- and women-owned businesses.[6]

Moreover, we interviewed officials from organizations that represent minority- and women-owned businesses such as the U.S. Hispanic Chamber of Commerce, the Pan Asian American Chamber of Commerce, National Black Chamber of Commerce, and the National Association of Women Business Owners. In addition, we interviewed officials from organizations that examine access to capital issues, such as the Milken Institute and the Kauffman Foundation.

We conducted our work from July 2005 to May 2006 in Washington, D.C., and New York City and in accordance with generally accepted government auditing standards.

APPENDIX II: OVERALL STATISTICS ON WORKFORCE DIVERSITY IN THE FINANCIAL SERVICES INDUSTRY

This appendix provides Employer Information Report (EEO-1) data on the number of employees within the financial services industry by position (see fig. 6) and more specific breakouts of the various racial/ethnic groups by position (see fig. 7).

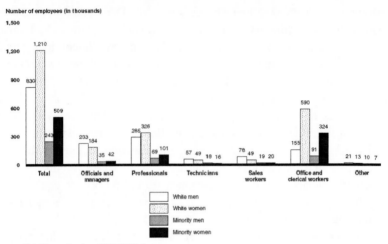

Source: GAO analysis of EEOC data.

Figure 6. EEO-1 Data (Number of Employees) on Workforce Diversity in the
Financial Services Industry by Position, Racial/Ethnic Group, and Gender (2004).

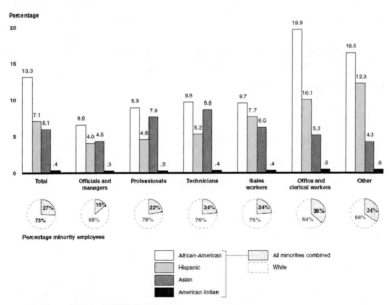

Source: GAO analysis of EEOC data.
Note: Percentages may not always add exactly due to rounding.

Figure 7. EEO-1 Data on Workforce Diversity in the Financial Services Industry by
Position and Racial/Ethnic Group (2004).

APPENDIX III: DIVERSITY IN KEY POSITIONS IN THE ACCOUNTING INDUSTRY

This appendix discusses workforce diversity of management-level positions in the accounting industry for 2004 as depicted by Employer Information Report (EEO-1) data. Additionally, it describes the findings of a report by the American Institute of Certified Public Accountants (AICPA) that assessed diversity within the accounting industry in a broad range of positions. Finally, the appendix summarizes efforts by AICPA and a large accounting firm to increase diversity in key positions.

Minorities Account for 14 Percent of Management-Level Positions in the Accounting Industry

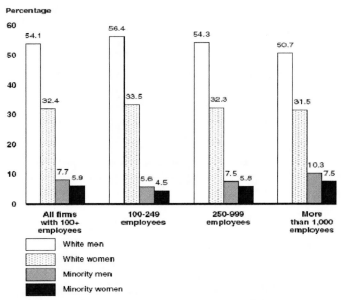

Source: GAO analysis of EEOC data..

Note: Percentages may not always add to 100 due to rounding.

Figure 8. EEO-1 Data on Workforce Diversity in the Accounting Industry at the Management Level by Firm Size, Gender, and Racial/Ethnic Group, and Gender (2004).

According to the 2004 EEO-1 data, minorities held 13.5 percent (5.9 percent for minority women and 7.7 percent for minority men) of all "officials and managers" positions, white women held 32.4 percent while white men held 54.1 percent of all official and manager positions in the accounting industry (see fig. 8).[1]

Contrary to the financial services sector where diversity among firms generally did not vary by firm size, EEO-1 data also show that larger accounting firms are in general more diverse than smaller firms. For example, minorities accounted for 17.8 percent of all officials and managers in accounting firms with 1,000 or more employees. For firms with 100 to 249 employees, minority representation for officials and managers accounted for 10.1 percent.

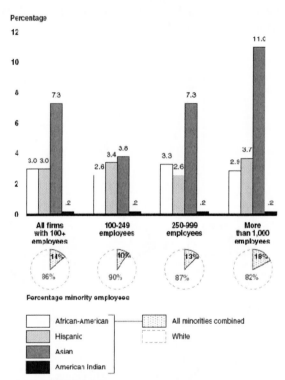

Source: GAO analysis of EEOC data.

Note: Percentages may not always add exactly due to rounding.

Figure 9. EEO-1 Data on Workforce Diversity in the Accounting Industry at the Management Level by Firm Size and Racial/Ethnic Group (2004).

Within the minority category in the accounting industry, EEO-1 2004 data show that Asians held 7.3 percent of all management-level positions, which is more than the representation of African-Americans (3.0 percent) and Hispanics (3.0 percent) combined (see fig. 9).

AICPA Study Identified a Lack of Diversity in the Accounting Industry

AICPA's 2005 demographic study showed that, in 2004, minorities represented 10 percent of all professional staff, 8 percent of all certified public accountants (CPA), and 5 percent of all partners/owners employed by CPA firms.[2] Correspondingly, the representation of whites among professional staff, CPAs, and the partner/owner level at accounting firms were all at 89 percent or above (see table 2).[3] In addition, consistent to the 2004 EEO-1 data for the accounting industry, the AICPA study found that the largest CPA firms were, in general, the most ethnically and racially diverse (see table 3).[4]

Table 2. Workforce Representation at the Professional, CPA and Partner/Owner Levels by Racial/Ethnic Group (2005)

Gender and racial/ethnic group	Professional staff	CPA	Partner/owner
Minority	10%	8%	5%
African-American	2	1	1
Hispanic	3	3	2
Asian/Pacific Islander	5	4	2
American Indian	a	a	a
White	89	92	95
Other	1%	a	a

Source: GAO analysis of AICPA data.

Note: Percentages may not always add to 100 due to rounding. AICPA data are from The Supply of Accounting Graduates and the Demand for Public Accounting Recruits (2005).

[a]Less than 1 percent.

According to officials from AICPA and a large accounting firm we spoke with, one reason for the lack of diversity in key positions in the industry is that relatively few racial/ethnic minorities take the CPA exam and thus relatively few minorities are CPAs. According to the 2004 congressional testimony of an accounting professor, passing the CPA exam is critical for achieving senior management-level positions in the accounting industry.[5]

Table 3. Workforce Representation at the Professional Level by Racial/Ethnic Group and Firm Size

Gender and racial/ethnic group	More than 200 employees	50-200 employees	10-49 employees	Fewer than 10 employees	All CPA firms
Minority	18%	8%	8%	10%	10%
• African-American	3	2	2	2	2
• Hispanic	4	2	3	4	3
• Asian/Pacific Islander	11	4	3	4	5
• American Indian	a	a	a	a	a
Other	a	1	a	1	1
White	82	91	92	89	89
Other	a	1%	a	1%	1%

Source: GAO analysis of AICPA data.

Note: Percentages may not always add to 100 due to rounding. AICPA data is from *The Supply of Accounting Graduates and the Demand for Public Accounting Recruits* (2005).

[a]Less than 1 percent.

Efforts to Enhance Accounting Industry Diversity

According to officials we spoke with from AICPA and an accounting firm, similar to the financial services industry, the accounting industry had also initiated programs to promote the diversity of its workforce. An official from the large accounting firm we spoke with told us that his firm's top management is committed to workforce diversity and has implemented a minority leadership development program, which ensures that minorities and women become eligible for and are recommended for progressively more senior positions. As part of the commitment to workforce diversity, the firm also has a mentoring program, which pairs current partners with senior management-level minority and women staff to help them achieve partnership status. In addition, the firm also requires middle- and high-level managers to undergo diversity training to encourage an open dialogue around racial-ethnic and gender issues. An AICPA official said the organization formed a minority initiatives committee to promote workforce diversity with a number of initiatives to increase the number of minority accounting degree holders, such as scholarships for minority accounting students and accounting faculty development programs. AICPA also formed partnerships with several national minority accounting organizations such as the National Association of Black Accountants and the Association of Latino Professionals in Finance and Accounting to develop new programs to foster diversity within the workplace and the community.

End Notes

[1] *Diversity In the Financial Services Industry and Access to Capital for Minority Owned Businesses: Challenges and Opportunities*, Hearing Before the Subcommittee On Oversight and Investigations of the House Committee on Financial Services, 108th Cong. (2004).

[2] GAO, *Diversity Management: Expert-Identified Leading Practices and Agency Examples*, GAO-05-90 (Washington, D.C.: Jan. 14, 2005).

[3] Generally, private employers with fewer than 100 employees and certain federal contractors who employ fewer than 50 employees are not required to submit EEO-1 reports to EEOC. Although the EEO-1 data do not include these smaller firms, the data do allow for the characterization of workforce diversity for firms with 100 or more employees due to EEOC's annual reporting requirement.

[4] U.S. Department of Commerce, Minority Business Development Agency, "Expanding Financing Opportunities for Minority Businesses" (2004).

[5] The Equal Credit Opportunity Act (ECOA), 15 U.S.C. §§ 1691-1691f, makes it unlawful for a creditor to discriminate against an applicant in any aspect of a credit transaction on the basis of the applicant's national origin, religion, sex, color, race, age (provided the applicant has the capacity to contract). Racial and gender information can be collected in two very limited circumstances, neither of which results in publicly available data regarding the race/ethnicity or gender of the bank's nonmortgage credit applicants.

[6] See U.S. Census Bureau, *National Population Projections* (January 2001).

[7] U.S. Census Bureau, *American Community Survey* (2004).

[8] U.S. Census Bureau, *Survey of Business Owners: Hispanic-Owned Firms: 2002* (March 2006).

[9] GAO-05-90.

[10] Our review did not attempt to define appropriate benchmarks for assessing the extent of management level diversity within the financial services industry and, instead, focused on changes in representation over time. While some analyses compare minority or gender representation in job categories or industries with general population statistics, such studies have limitations. For example, such analyses do not account for the educational attainment, age, or experience requirements, among many others, that may be necessary for particular positions, including management-level positions within the financial services industry. Further, we did not identify a feasible means to comprehensively adjust available population or labor force data based on the qualification requirements (e.g., education and experience) for management-level positions in the financial services industry due to the large number of such positions and their related qualification requirements. Such adjustments would have to be made to determine the relevant civilian labor force against

which to assess the management-level diversity with the financial services industry. However, the report does discuss some potential management requirements, such as holding a Masters of Business Administration degree.

[11] See Securities Industry Association, *2005 Report on Diversity Strategy, Development and Demographics: Executive Summary* (November 2005). The study also found that total representation of minorities and women increased between 2001 and 2005.

[12] For example, for the holdings and trust sector, the share of positions held by white women are higher in firms with more than 1,000 employees than smaller firms.

[13] SIA (2005). Unlike our analysis, the study of 48 securities firms included positions such as assistants, analysts and associates, mid-level positions, senior-level positions, retail brokers, and institutional sales staff.

[14] AACSB, the world's largest accreditation association for business schools, conducts an annual survey called "Business School Questionnaire" of all its accredited schools. Participation in this survey is voluntary. For the year 2004, the most recent year, 92.7 percent of the accredited schools responded to the survey.

[15] GMAC® has been conducting its "Global MBA Graduate Survey" since 2000. To obtain the demographic data for 2004, GMAC® mailed out 18,504 surveys to graduating MBA students with a response rate of 34 percent.

[16] See EEOC, *Diversity in the Finance Industry* (April 2006). In the study, EEOC analyzed the 2003 EEO-1 data by an analytical technique referred to as odds-ratio analysis to assess the potential chances of minorities and women becoming managers as compared with white men. The analysis assumes the pipeline for "officials and managers" job category generally consists of professionals. However, the study also included "sales workers" as a potential pool of managers in some analyses because in the securities sector, stock brokers might become managers, according to EEOC.

[17] For example, EEOC said that the EEO-1 data do not show how many employees are promoted from one job group to another over time, and so promotion data are not available. Rather, the EEO-1 survey collects information on the number of employees in various job categories at a given point in time. In the absence of promotion data, EEOC views the analysis as a screening tool to identify potential disparities.

[18] A minority-owned business is defined by Census as a business in which a minority owns 51 percent or more of the stock or equity in the business. A woman-owned business is defined by Census as a business in which a woman owns 51 percent or more of the stock or equity in the business.

[19] Equity capital can be raised from several sources including venture capital funds, private stock sales, or issuing stock in public financial markets.

[20] It should be noted that all small businesses may face challenges in obtaining credit due to the risks and costs involved in such lending. See Board of Governors of the Federal Reserve System, *Report to the Congress on the Availability of Credit to Small Businesses* (September 2002).

[21] U.S. Department of Commerce, Minority Business Development Agency, *Expanding Financing Opportunities for Minority Businesses* (2004). U.S. Department of Commerce, Minority Business Development Agency, *Keys to Minority Entrepreneurial Success, Capital, Education, and Technology* (September 2002). U.S. Department of Commerce, Minority Business Development Agency, *State of Minority Business Enterprises: A Preliminary Overview of the 2002 Survey of Business Owners* (September 2005).

[22] U.S. Department of Commerce, Minority Business Development Agency, *State of Minority Business Enterprises: A Preliminary Overview of the 2002 Survey of Business Owners*

(September 2005). U. S. Census Bureau, "2002 Survey of Business Owners, Women-Owned Firms" (Jan. 26, 2006).

[23] U.S. Department of Commerce, Minority Business Development Agency, *Keys to Minority Entrepreneurial Success, Capital, Education, and Technology* (September 2002). U.S. Small Business Administration, Office of Advocacy, *Financing Patterns of Small Firms: Findings from the 1998 Survey of Small Business Finance* (September 2003).

[24] U.S. Department of Commerce, Minority Business Development Agency, *Expanding Financing Opportunities for Minority Businesses* (2004).

[25] U.S. Small Business Administration, *The Small Business Economy* (Washington, D.C.: 2005).

[26] Blanchard, Lloyd, John Yinger, and Bo Zhao (2005), "Do Credit Market Barriers Exist for Minority and Women Entrepreneurs?" Syracuse University, Center for Policy Research Working Paper No. 74. Blanchflower, David G, P. Levine, and D. Zimmerman (1998). "Discrimination in the Small Business Credit Market", National Bureau of Economic Research. Cavalluzzo, Ken and John Wolken (2002). "Small Business Loan Turndowns, Personal Wealth and Discrimination. Georgetown University." Coleman, Susan (2002). "Characteristics and Borrowing Behavior of Small, Women-Owned Firms: Evidence from the 1998 National Survey of Small Business Finances." University of Hartford.

[27] Blanchard, Lloyd, John Yinger, and Bo Zhao (2005), "Do Credit Market Barriers Exist for Minority and Women Entrepreneurs?" Syracuse University, Center for Policy Research Working Paper No. 74.

[28] Cavalluzzo, Ken and John Wolken (2002). "Small Business Loan Turndowns, Personal Wealth and Discrimination." Georgetown University.

[29] U.S. Small Business Administration (2005). *Availability of Financing to Small Firms Using the Survey of Small Business Finances*. A report for the U.S. Small Business Administration, Washington, D.C.

[30] Relationship loans are defined as a commitment by the lender to a pre-set maximum amount of credit over a certain time period. Transaction loans are injections of cash made after loan approval and used to acquire tangible assets that can serve as loan collateral.

[31] See Small Business Administration (2005).

[32] The Equal Credit Opportunity Act (ECOA), 15 U.S.C. §§ 1691-1691f.

[33] Milken Institute, *The Minority Business Challenge: Democratizing Capital for Emerging Domestic Markets* (September 2000).

[34] Center for Women's Business Research, *Access to Capital: Where We've Been, Where We're Going* (March 2005).

[35] Center for Women's Business Research, *Access to Capital: Where We've Been, Where We're Going* (March 2005). Brush, C. G.; Carter, N.; Gatewood, E.; Greene P. G.; and Hart, M. M. *Gatekeepers of Venture Growth: A Diana Project Report on the Role and Participation of Women in the Venture Capital Industry* (Oct. 20, 2001).

[36] Bates, Timothy and William Bradford (2003). "Minorities and Venture Capital, A New Wave in American Business." Kauffman Foundation.

End Notes for Appendix I

[1] Federal contractors with 50 or more employees are also required to report EEO-1 data. However, we did not include these firms in our analysis. See 29 C.F.R. Part 1602, Subpart B.

[2] See Securities Industry Association, *2005 Report on Diversity Strategy, Development and Demographics: Executive Summary* (November 2005).

[3] We considered using data from Census' Current Population Survey (CPS), Public Use Microdata Sample (PUMS), Special EEO Tabulation File, and the American Community Survey (ACS). The CPS is reported by individuals and includes smaller employers, and the PUMS is reported by households; however due to small sample sizes, reliable estimates to specific minority groups could not be derived. The Special EEO Tabulation File's most recent data are based on the 2000 census and thus were more dated than other data sources. The ACS only has data since 2002 and therefore did not allow us to show shifts over a large span of time.

[4] EEOC implemented the NAICS in 2002.

[5] Equal Employment Opportunity Commission, *Diversity in the Finance Industry* (April 2006).

[6] Banks included national, community, minority-owned banks, and one women-owned bank. We also selected the firms based on our interviews with organizations that represent minority- and women-owned businesses. We were seeking firms that may have initiatives to assist minority- and women-owned businesses in obtaining capital.

End Notes for Appendix III

[1] Percentages may not always add exactly due to rounding.

[2] AICPA, *The Supply of Accounting Graduates And the Demand for Public Accounting Recruits – 2005 For Academic Year 2003-2004* (2005). AICPA surveyed 5,821 certified public accounting firms, and 1,423 responded.

[3] AICPA's study did not report representation levels of whites and minorities by gender.

[4] The largest firms are defined as those with more than 200 members.

[5] *Diversity in the Financial Services Industry and Access to Capital for Minority Owned Businesses: Challenges and Opportunities*, Hearing before the Subcommittee On Oversight and Investigations of the House Committee on Financial Services, 108th Cong (2004).

INDEX

F

G

H